D1024703

Praise for
Morning Moments with God

"*Morning Moments with God* is a treasure of a devotional! If you are a busy woman who has little time but you know you need a daily dose of inspiration from biblical truth, this is the ideal resource for you! Buy one for yourself and ten more to give away. I love this book!"

Carol Kent
speaker and author of *When I Lay My Isaac Down*

"In *Morning Moments with God*, Grace Fox shares wisdom from God's Word that is sure to make your day brighter. Each wonderful wake-up inspiration will get you started on a great day!"

Pam Farrel
author of *Becoming a Brave New Woman*
and coauthor of *Devotions for Women on the Go*

"Each reading is brief but powerful, inspirational, and practical. Uplifting, challenging, convicting! What a great way to start the day!"

Christin Ditchfield
author, speaker, and host of *Take It to Heart!*

"Grace pulls treasure after treasure from her Bible, setting them in the mosaic of current, real-life experiences. I love that each devotional leads me to action and then leaves me in anticipation of tomorrow's inspiration and challenge."

Donna Lamothe
Executive Director, Stonecroft Canada

"In *Morning Moments with God*, Grace Fox artfully expresses the questions and struggles that have puzzled the human heart since time began. Her honest and often inspired stories invite us to a more intimate daily walk with Jesus, the lover of our souls and the answer to every prayer. I know busy women like me will be encouraged by these brief but brilliant reminders of God's faithfulness."

Marilee Pierce Dunker
World Vision ambassador for children

Morning
Moments
with GOD

Grace Fox

HARVEST HOUSE PUBLISHERS
EUGENE, OREGON

Cover by Dugan Design Group, Bloomington, Minnesota

Cover photo © Route 16 / Fotolia

Grace Fox is published in association with the literary agency of The Steve Laube Agency, LLC, 5025 N. Central Ave., #635, Phoenix, Arizona, 85012.

MORNING MOMENTS WITH GOD
Copyright © 2014 by Grace Fox
Published by Harvest House Publishers
Eugene, Oregon 97402
www.harvesthousepublishers.com

ISBN 978-0-7369-5552-2 (Padded HC)
ISBN 978-0-7369-5553-9 (eBook)

Printed in China

13 14 15 16 17 18 19 20 21 / RDS-JH / 10 9 8 7 6 5 4 3 2 1

Thank You, God, for inviting relationship.
I'm eternally grateful.

My heart has heard you say, "Come and talk with me."
And my heart responds, "LORD, I am coming."
PSALM 27:8 NLT

Acknowledgments

Many deserve credit for bringing this book to reality. Terry Glaspey captured my vision and presented my proposal to the Harvest House team. Gene Skinner edited my work. Others helped polish the manuscript, develop the layout, and design the cover. My literary agent, Steve Laube, represented me well. Thank you, all, for your roles.

Thanks as well to those who prayed for me as I wrote. More than once I posted a note on Facebook—"Please pray me through." Response came immediately, and I felt it. A seniors' group at my church prayed diligently, as did my personal prayer team and countless other friends and family members. The importance of your role cannot be overestimated.

Thank you to my personal cheerleading squad—son Matthew and his wife Cheryl, daughter Stephanie and her husband Daniel, daughter Kim, and grandkids Anna, Luke, Caleb, and Simon. I love you. Fix your hearts on Jesus, and everything else will fall into place.

And finally, gratitude overflows to my husband, Gene. You're truly God's gift. Thank you for modeling servanthood to me throughout the writing process—bringing lattes midafternoon, doing laundry, preparing meals, and more. Thank you for sacrificing time and energy. God did something good when He made us a team.

May these combined efforts bless you, and may God receive the glory.

In the morning, Lord, you hear my voice;
in the morning I lay my requests before you
and wait expectantly.

PSALM 5:3

Today Is a Gift

Lord, thank You for this and every day.

This is the day the Lord has made. We will rejoice and be glad in it," says Psalm 118:24 (NLT). These words resonate with us some days more than others. Do you agree?

Our family recently vacationed at a lakefront cabin. Waking up to water-ski and play on the beach made it easy to rejoice. Returning home to chores—not so much.

Regardless of our feelings, the truth remains—today is a gift not to be wished away for tomorrow or overlooked with yearnings for yesterday. Open it with anticipation. Expect to experience God's presence and love.

I start each morning with this Scripture. Before I roll from bed, I say, "This is the day You've made, Lord. I'll rejoice and be glad in it." This sets me in a healthy place, and I'm more apt to respond in a God-honoring way come what may.

Consider adopting my habit unless you already have a similar one that works for you. Whatever you do, regard today as God's gift. Embrace it, for it will never pass this way again.

Take Action: Say aloud, "This is the day You've made, Lord. I will rejoice and celebrate!"

The Weapon of Praise

Lord, teach me to praise at all times.

What's your usual response when discouragement strikes? Do you withdraw? Share your concerns with a friend? Nibble on the nearest comfort food?

Discouragement affects different people in different ways. Regardless, God has given us a weapon to break its grip. That weapon is praise.

"Praise is an adventure—an empowering adventure," writes Michael Youssef. "Praise is more than an obligation, more than a spiritual exercise. Praise is the path that brings us near to God and His love, His power, and His grace."[1]

Drawing near to God through praise results in a changed perspective. Burdens lighten as we see Him as the source of all strength. Sorrow eases as we recognize Him as the comforter. Confusion fades as we acknowledge Him as our source of wisdom. And joy increases as we hail Him for His unfailing love and faithfulness.

"You who fear the LORD, praise him!" says the psalmist (Psalm 22:23). Let's do it. Let's praise God daily for who He is, and even more when discouragement strikes.

Take Action: Fill in the blank: "God, I praise You for
_____."

Divine Details

*Lord, Your command over the details
of my life amazes me.*

God is masterful at aligning details to accomplish
His purposes. Ruth's story illustrates this well.

Ruth and Naomi arrived in Bethlehem as barley
season began. One day Ruth (a young widow) went out
to glean grain. Unknowingly, she chose a field belonging to Boaz (a distant relative and eligible bachelor). Lo
and behold! Boaz showed up at the field on the same
day, and the rest is history. The couple became part of
Christ's lineage (Ruth 1:22–2:4).

Uniting Ruth and Boaz was no small feat considering the potential variables. Naomi and Ruth's arrival
in Bethlehem might have fallen after barley harvest. Or
Ruth might have chosen a field belonging to a different
man. Or Boaz might have shown up a day late.

But no. Every detail fell into place by divine direction.

Do you believe God can align details to accomplish
His purposes for your life? He can, and He will. Resist
the urge to manipulate. He doesn't need your help; He
wants your trust.

Take Action: Write a prayer inviting God to align every
detail of your life to accomplish His purposes. Ask Him
to demonstrate His amazing power.

Divine Details and Second Thoughts

Lord, teach me to trust when I don't understand.

The details of Ruth's life played like a fairy tale. Young widow meets rich landowner, falls in love, marries, and has a family. The details of Joseph's life looked much different. He was sold into slavery at age 17, falsely accused of rape by his master's wife, and locked in prison for an unjust accusation.

Perhaps Joseph felt as if God had written the details of his life on a piece of scrap paper and then trashed it. In reality, the opposite was true.

Scripture says God was with Joseph throughout his ordeal. God's purpose involved establishing him as a leader in Egypt so he could save many lives during a seven-year famine, but Joseph didn't know this at the time. He simply had to trust (Genesis 50:20).

Sometimes we don't understand why the details of our lives play out as they do. We may be tempted to doubt God's sovereignty and love. Let's choose instead to pray, remember His promises, and persevere, knowing that He sees a bigger picture than we see.

Take Action: Recall a lesson you've learned through difficult circumstances in your life.

Help, Please

Lord, thank You for hearing simple prayers.

Thank heaven God honors simple prayers.

My husband and I had spent two weeks ministering to HIV-infected youth in Romania. When our time there ended, we headed to Poland to host an evangelistic family camp.

I was already tired, and traveling by bus for several hours in scorching heat drained my remaining energy. Sweat trickled down my face, chest, and back. When two hours yet remained, I seriously doubted my ability to go on. That's when I prayed a simple, desperate prayer: "God, will You help me, please?"

He answered. He didn't send cooler weather or air conditioning, but He gave me the oomph I needed to complete the trip.

Psalm 86:6-7 says, "Hear my prayer, LORD; listen to my cry for mercy. When I am in distress, I call to you, because you answer me."

God promises to respond when we call on Him. Our prayers needn't be long or fancy. The simple prayer, "Help, please," uttered with childlike faith, is enough.

Take Action: What's your need today? Go ahead—pray a simple prayer asking for help.

The Shepherd's Promise

Lord, thank You for promising to meet my needs.

My fiftieth birthday dawned with great anticipation. I grabbed a cup of coffee, my Bible, and my journal, and I headed to the backyard for quiet time with Jesus.

"Please give me a promise that's good for the next 50 years," I prayed. Instantly a familiar Bible reference popped into my head—Psalm 23:1. "Thanks, but that one's too ordinary," I said. "I'd like something more unique, please."

The reference stuck, so I pondered its words. "The LORD is my Shepherd, I lack nothing." Their meaning left me in awe.

Imagine—God, as my Shepherd, assumes responsibility for my well-being. He gives me everything I need. Everything. How amazing is that? Comfort comes and peace presides when I bask in this truth.

This promise is for you too, my friend. Rest assured that the good Shepherd knows what your needs are today and has promised to provide. He cares about your well-being. You will lack nothing. Nothing! How amazing is that?

Take Action: List your needs on paper. (Be sure not to confuse needs with wants.) Now thank the Lord for being your Shepherd and for promising to meet those needs.

A Different Standard

Lord, make my mind like Yours.

"Follow your heart"—have you heard this phrase? It sounds innocent, but imagine the hurt we would endure if we lived according to this pseudo-truth...

A married woman, enamored with a guy she met online, leaves her family. A single gal intentionally gets pregnant to satisfy her longing for a child. A woman eats whatever she craves regardless of its negative impact on her health.

Who's to say they're making poor choices? They're just following their hearts.

Scripture warns us not to think the way the world does. "Do not conform to the pattern of this world, but be transformed by the renewing of your mind. Then you will be able to test and approve what God's will is—his good, pleasing and perfect will" (Romans 12:2).

God renews and transforms our minds as we fill them with the truth of His word. This makes us alert to thought patterns that sound good but are based on emotion. It also enables us to live purposefully and without regret.

Follow your heart, but first make sure your heart conforms to God's truth.

Take Action: Memorize Romans 12:2.

Loving the Naomi

Lord, please love prickly people through me.

Naomi was a widow living in a foreign land. When death claimed her husband and two grown sons, she chose to return to her homeland. Her two daughters-in-law offered to move with her, but she said no. Life had dealt a cruel blow, and she felt bitter. Her misery did not want company.

One daughter-in-law, Ruth, refused to accept the no. "Where you go I will go, and where you stay I will stay," she said. Now *that's* love, especially considering Naomi's bitter state (Ruth 1:16).

Bitter women remind me of cactus plants. I'm tempted to think twice before hugging one, but not so Ruth. She willingly loved the prickly lady, and God honored her for doing so.

Follow Ruth's example by loving the Naomi in your life. She may be a family member, a coworker, a neighbor, a business associate, or someone who attends your church. She may be older than you, younger, or a peer. Regardless of specifics, she's a lady who needs love. Let's be willing to give it.

Take Action: Name the Naomi in your life. Think of a way to show her your love in one tangible way this week.

God Speaks

Lord, tune my ear to hear Your voice.

Driving alone gave me an opportunity to listen to my favorite radio station and sing along with gusto. Suddenly a voice from within interrupted my fun.

"Turn off the music."

"Naw," I protested. "I'm having a good time!"

"Turn it off."

I knew it was God. I switched off the radio, and silence filled my car.

This is what I heard next: "You're my daughter, and I'm well pleased with you." I'm a woman of words, but that moment rendered me speechless.

God longs to communicate with us. Sometimes He speaks in an audible voice. Sometimes in whispers. He can speak through a sermon, a poem, a favorite song, a child's observations, and a senior's recollections.

God's methods of speaking are myriad. Do we expect to hear Him? Do we recognize His voice when it comes? Do we quiet ourselves and listen?

Let's live today with anticipation, knowing God wants to speak with us. Let's make Samuel's words our motto: "Speak, for your servant is listening" (1 Samuel 3:10).

Take Action: Ask God to make you keenly aware of His whispers today.

Sharing Christ

*Lord, enable me to talk about You
with grace and boldness.*

Why are we quick to recommend doctors who heal us physically but sometimes reluctant to recommend the One who offers spiritual healing?

Evangelism can be difficult. No doubt fear plays a role—fear of being labeled a religious fanatic, of offending someone with differing views, of stumbling over our words, and of rejection.

Fear is big, but we can alleviate it by remembering this truth: Convicting people of sin and their need for Christ is not our job. That's the Holy Spirit's role.

Our job is to tactfully tell what Christ has done for us. We need not feel embarrassed or apologetic. We simply need to say what we've experienced and, in doing so, introduce the One who's brought healing and hope.

The apostle Paul said, "I am not ashamed of the gospel, because it is the power of God that brings salvation to everyone who believes" (Romans 1:16). He boldly proclaimed Christ. Let's ask God to give us the courage to do likewise.

Take Action: Pray for an opportunity to speak about Christ to someone today.

A Painful Past

*Lord, thank You for assuring me that my past
doesn't dictate my future.*

"You need to know something about me," said a
woman I'd met a few months prior. Tears welled in
her eyes. "I've had two abortions. I'm so ashamed. Will
I ever move beyond my past? Can God use me despite
what I've done?"

No one has a pristine past. Satan loves to remind
us of this fact. He dupes us into believing we're dam-
aged goods. Forever scarred. Dirty. Broken. Worthless.

But Scripture says otherwise. "If anyone is in Christ,
the new creation has come: The old has gone, the new
is here!" (2 Corinthians 5:17).

The Bible also says God gives us beauty for ashes
(Isaiah 61:3). Christ cleanses us from sin, removes our
guilt, and then wonderfully allows us to use our difficult life lessons to help others struggling with similar
issues. Our most effective ministry often flows from our
deepest pain if we make ourselves available.

God knows everything about our past and loves us
anyway. Let's trust Him to heal our wounds and then use
us to encourage others so they can experience healing too.

Take Action: Read Zephaniah 3:17. What is God's opinion of you?

Hang On Tight

Lord, I need You at all times.

Waves slapped our boat as we shoved off the dock. "This will be fun!" said my three-year-old grandson, Luke. He climbed onto my lap.

My husband revved the engine, and a panicked expression crossed Luke's face. He grabbed my arms and pulled them around his torso. "Hold me tight!"

Luke clung to me until we approached the shore 15 minutes later. As the motor quieted, his body relaxed. So did his attitude. "Are we going slow now?" he asked.

"Yes," I replied.

"Then I don't need you." Ouch.

How often do we model the same behavior toward God? We cling to Him until the waves settle and the wind dies. Our fear subsides, and we grow comfortable without Him.

Such was the Israelites' pattern (Nehemiah 9:27-28). When life was easy, they wandered from God. But when circumstances took a negative turn, they begged Him for help.

Let's learn to revel in God's closeness at all times, not just when we're feeling insecure. God is faithful through thick and thin. Let's respond in kind.

Take Action: Invite God to create in you a craving for closeness with Him at all times.

The Serpent's Tactic

*Lord, teach me more about who You are
so I will doubt You less.*

Satan aims to destroy us. One of his favorite ploys is to cast doubt on God's character, as he did with Eve. The conversation in Genesis 3 went something like this.

"Did God really say, 'You mustn't eat from any tree in the garden'?" Satan asked.

"We can eat from every tree except the tree of the knowledge of good and evil," said Eve. "Even touching it will bring death."

"You won't die," said Satan. "God knows that when you eat from it, your eyes will be opened, and you'll be like Him, knowing good and evil."

In so few words, Satan made God look dubious to Eve. Doubt led to distrust, disobedience, spiritual disconnection, and ultimately death.

We can thwart Satan's ploy by filling our minds with the truth about God's character. This reinforces our trust in Him, enables us to believe His promises, and strengthens our courage to obey what He commands. We become formidable forces in God's kingdom, and that's the last thing Satan wants.

Know God's character—that's the key to victory.

Take Action: When fear haunts you, ask yourself, "What aspect of God's character am I doubting?"

One Thing

Lord, please grant me this one desire.

Imagine a genie suddenly appears. He says, "I'll grant you one wish. Make it good. You have ten seconds to think about it. Ten…nine…eight…"

This scene is only make-believe, but it's worth pondering. What one thing would we desire the most? Financial security? World peace? Perfect health?

How about a great marriage, good family relationships, freedom to travel, or three extra hours in each day?

Honestly, all those ideas sound enticing. But they don't even come close to the psalmist's one thing. He wrote, "One thing I ask from the LORD, this only do I seek: that I may dwell in the house of the LORD all the days of my life, to gaze upon the beauty of the LORD and to seek him in his temple" (Psalm 27:4).

The psalmist got it right—intimacy with God is the thing that matters most. Material possessions fade and people fail us, but our relationship with God equips us for this life, and it lasts forever. Choose it above all else.

Take Action: Fill in the blank: "If I could have one wish granted, I would wish for _____."

Perfectionism

Lord, thanks for loving me unconditionally.

Snip, snip, snip. I examined the paper heart in my hand, spied a jagged edge, and snipped again. "Oh-oh," I thought. "It's crooked. I have to make it even." And so went my first-grade craft until my teacher stopped me.

"What have you done?" she asked. "Your shape is too small now. Start over."

The criticism devastated me. My efforts to produce a perfect valentine had failed.

Perfectionism trapped me for decades. I feared failing and disappointing others, including God. It didn't help that Jesus said, "Be perfect, therefore, as your heavenly Father is perfect" (Matthew 5:48).

Thankfully, the truth dawned. I began to understand that Jesus wasn't telling us to perform flawlessly. He was encouraging us to pursue spiritual maturity and exemplify the same character attributes as God. He doesn't expect us to do this on our own. He works in us to accomplish this goal.

Are you a perfectionist? Acknowledge your fear of failure. Ask God to help you understand His unconditional love for you. Invest time in your friendship with Him, and you'll find freedom.

Take Action: Identify behaviors in your life that are rooted in perfectionism.

Lavish Gifts

Lord, Your lavish gifts leave me speechless.

God is a lavish gift-giver. That's right! "In him we have redemption through his blood, the forgiveness of sins, in accordance with the riches of God's grace that he lavished on us" (Ephesians 1:7-8).

My dictionary defines "lavish" this way: "to bestow something in generous or extravagant quantities upon." According to this definition, God is the opposite of skimpy. He showers His favor on His children. He begins with the free gift of salvation and then pours out on us everything we need to live victoriously.

What do you need to live victoriously today? Patience with your kids? Strength to care for an aging parent or special-needs child? Courage to face an unknown future?

Do you need comfort? Perseverance? Wisdom?

Perhaps you need joy. Or self-discipline to care properly for your body as God's temple.

Tell God what you need today. Pray in confidence. Believe He will answer, and thank Him in advance for His lavish gifts. Everything you need, He will supply extravagantly.

Take Action: Fill in the blank: "God, today I need _____ to live victoriously. Thank You for providing lavishly. Amen."

Facing an Army

Lord, please show me what to do.

News of an impending attack from neighboring territories drove King Jehoshaphat to his knees. "We have no power to face this vast army that is attacking us," he prayed. "We do not know what to do, but our eyes are on you."

No fancy words, no long-winded monologue. Just simple statements of fact: We're in trouble. We don't know what to do. We need Your help.

How did God respond? He answered by fighting the battle on Jehoshaphat's behalf and giving victory (2 Chronicles 20:12-22).

Have you ever faced a vast army, so to speak, feeling utterly powerless? Maybe you're in an abusive relationship. Perhaps you're heartbroken over wayward kids. Maybe you're struggling with depression, facing financial ruin, or battling terminal illness. The army approaches, and you see no escape. What to do? Pray.

"I don't know what to do, but my eyes are on You."

You may feel powerless, but God is all-powerful. Rest assured, He'll fight on your behalf just as He did for Jehoshaphat.

Take Action: Fill in the blank: "God, I don't know what to do about _____, but my eyes are on You."

Spontaneous Worship

Lord, thank You for filling my heart with joy.

My husband and I had just returned from a month overseas, and our grandkids were ecstatic to see us. Anna, then age four, chattered about a recent camping trip, picking blueberries, and shopping with her mom. Her joy bubbled and spilled over. Suddenly she burst into a love song to Jesus.

Psalm 28:7 says, "The LORD is my strength and my shield; my heart trusts in him, and he helps me. My heart leaps for joy, and with my song I praise him."

The New Living Translation renders this verse, "He helps me, and my heart is filled with joy. I burst out in songs of thanksgiving."

When was the last time your heart couldn't contain the love and gratitude you felt for Jesus? When was the last time your joy bubbled over and you burst into song?

Take time today to count your blessings. Consider God's promises. Realize afresh His unfailing love for you.

And then sing, sister, sing!

Take Action: Turn Psalm 28:7 into a song and sing it to the Lord.

Never Give Up

Lord, please grant me strength to persevere.

Have you ever wrestled with a difficult relationship, trying to make things work but to no avail? Have you ever felt like throwing your hands in the air and walking away after fruitless efforts?

You've used kind words and deeds to draw a smile, thaw the ice, and remove the prickles. You've invested time and energy, but change is slow in coming.

I'm not a psychologist, but I've been around long enough to see some people as the walking wounded. Others have trust issues or struggle with fear or unforgiveness. Some may need professional counsel before they can enjoy healthy relationships. Others will warm and respond to kindness over time.

God puts difficult people into our lives for a reason. Honor Him by obeying Galatians 6:9—"Let us not become weary in doing good, for at the proper time we will reap a harvest if we do not give up."

Persevere, my friend. Do not grow weary of doing good even if your efforts seem unnoticed. God sees your persistence, and He'll reward you.

Take Action: Today, do a simple act of kindness for a difficult person you know.

Attitude Check

Lord, please enable me to live complaint free.

Granny Maude was a sweetie. I can still picture her weeding the church flowerbed. "We want to keep it lookin' nice," she'd say, adding her signature giggle.

Widowed decades before we met, Maude raised her kids alone. Later she cleaned other people's houses and invested in her grandchildren's lives. She invested in mine too—teaching me how to preserve fruit and babysitting my kids periodically.

During the 25 years I knew Maude, I never heard her complain. She spoke words of encouragement, expressed gratitude for life's simple pleasures, and cheerfully went about her business.

"Do everything without grumbling or arguing," says Philippians 2:14. That's a tall order, especially when life deals harsh blows. But God commands, and the indwelling Holy Spirit empowers. Maude proves it.

Let's seek to honor God with our attitude. Let's do all things without complaining or arguing regardless of what comes our way. We may have to undo old habits or ask someone to hold us accountable, but that's okay. Let's do what's necessary to ensure we're walking according to God's word.

Take Action: For the next month, put a dime in a jar each time you complain or argue.

A Lesson from the Mountains

*Lord, thanks for giving me a glimpse of
Your power through creation.*

Flying between London and Vancouver several
times each year allows me to view Greenland's rugged mountains. I never tire of seeing their peaks. They
remind me of Psalm 121:1-2—"I look up to the mountains—does my help come from there? My help comes
from the Lord, who made heaven and earth!" (NLT).

Mountains appear daunting. They stand like
mighty warriors, daring anyone to scale their heights.
And yet their strength is nothing compared to the
mighty power of God, who created them.

When I'm fearful or weary, I look to the mountains
towering near my city and remember that the God who
made them cares for me. He promises to keep me from
stumbling. He stays awake to watch over me and to
protect me from evil (Psalm 121:3-8). Courage fills me,
and comfort restores me.

The next time you feel afraid, look to or imagine
the mountains and their mighty presence. Then give
thanks to the One who created them for being stronger and being on your side.

Take Action: Post a picture of mountains on your fridge
to remind you that their Creator helps you.

Three Little Words

Lord, I praise You because You can do the impossible.

Pharaoh experienced disturbing dreams one night. His wise men couldn't interpret their meaning, so he asked Joseph to explain. Joseph said, "I cannot do it...but God will give Pharaoh the answer he desires" (Genesis 41:16).

Joseph could have said, "You want me to do *what*? Sorry, I can't do that." Period.

Instead, he acknowledged his powerlessness and then proceeded to trust God for the words to say. Three little words spoken in faith—"but God will"—moved him from the prison to the palace. They contain the same life-changing power today.

- "I can't forgive her for hurting me, but God will give me the grace I need."
- "I can't give thanks in my circumstances, but God will enable me to do what He commands."
- "I can't face an unknown future, but God will give me the strength I need."

Three little words—"but God will." Speak them in faith when you face an impossibility, and they can change your life.

Take Action: Fill in the blank: "It's beyond my power to _____, but God will do it."

Rest

Lord, teach me to slow down, to rest, to breathe.

To say life is busy is an understatement. Sometimes we sprint for a few weeks or months and then stop and catch our breath. Sometimes, however, we feel caught in a never-ending marathon.

Constant activity seems to be the accepted and even expected way of life in today's society. But is it what God intends for us? Maybe not. After all, even He rested on the seventh day.

Jesus knew the bane of busyness. He preached, healed the sick, raised the dead, restored sight to the blind, cast out demons, fed thousands, faced angry mobs, answered jealous leaders, and preached again. He filled His days with meaningful ministry, but in the midst, He acknowledged the need to recharge.

"Come with me by yourselves to a quiet place and get some rest," Jesus told His disciples after a particularly long day. Still the crowds pursued Him, but He later slipped into the hills alone to pray (Mark 6:31,45-46).

Rest refreshes body and soul. God rested. Jesus did too. Are you following His example?

Take Action: Spend five minutes doing nothing today. And don't feel guilty!

Interruptions

Lord, teach me to see the unforeseen as You do.

It's no surprise—our days seldom go as planned. Do we regard the unforeseen as annoying interruptions, or do we look for God's purposes in them?

My friend Barb has mastered the latter. Every morning she offers her time and to-do list to the Lord. When (not if) interruptions come, she thanks Him for controlling every detail of her day, and she asks what He has in mind so she can participate in His purposes. Her strategy works. God blesses people through her in amazing ways.

Proverbs 16:9 says, "In their hearts humans plan their course, but the LORD establishes their steps." This truth applies to the major decisions we make, but it also applies to everyday life. We make our plans, but the Lord determines the direction they take and the details involved.

Let's commit to viewing the unforeseen through God's eyes. Let's embrace whatever He brings and seek to partner with Him to accomplish His purposes.

Take Action: Take a moment now to give God complete control over your day.

My Greatest Joy

Lord, nothing compares to knowing You.

Joy comes to people in various ways. Some folks experience it in nature's beauty or in reading a good book. Others, like me, find it in hearing a baby's giggles.

I find joy in life's simple pleasures, but my deepest joy comes from knowing Jesus as my Savior. Each morning I rise early, nestle into my favorite love seat with open Bible and journal, and savor time with Him.

Psalm 4:6-7 (NLT) says, "Let your face smile on us, Lord. You have given me greater joy than those who have abundant harvests of grain and new wine."

This psalmist knew true joy. He also knew its source—the Lord. Relationship with Him brings greater joy than success, material abundance, or anything else we might imagine.

Here's why. In Christ we experience forgiveness, friendship, and fruitfulness. We find courage, comfort, healing, and hope for eternity. Other sources of joy come and go, but Christ and the blessings He gives remain the same.

What brings you joy? Go ahead and relish life's simple pleasures, but find your greatest joy in knowing Jesus.

Take Action: List five reasons why Jesus is your source of joy.

Holiness

Lord, make me holy.

God intends for mankind to be holy. That desire is woven throughout Scripture. "As obedient children, do not conform to the evil desires you had when you lived in ignorance. But just as he who called you is holy, so be holy in all you do; for it is written: 'Be holy, because I am holy'" (1 Peter 1:14-16).

Why is this so important? God wants us to be holy so we can enjoy intimacy with Him. As oil and water cannot mix, so we cannot enjoy friendship with the sinless One if we knowingly harbor sin in our lives.

God knows this standard is impossible for us to achieve on our own, so He provides the means through Christ's work on the cross and the indwelling Holy Spirit. But we have a role too. We're to surrender ourselves to Him, allowing Him to refine us, teach us, and grow us into His likeness.

Do you want intimacy with God? Partner with Him so you can be holy as He is holy.

Take Action: Name and confess unholy attitudes and actions in your life. Ask God for victory over them.

Bring 'Em Back

Lord, thank You for making inner peace possible.

My husband and I were sitting on our favorite love seat. A football game engrossed him; Facebook absorbed me.

Emotion surged through me when I glanced at Gene. "He's so wonderful," I thought. "I'd sure miss him if he died suddenly." Within seconds, I imagined breaking the tragic news to our kids and choosing songs for his memorial service.

I brushed a tear away and glanced at Gene again. There he sat, eating popcorn, oblivious to my sorrow. That's when I realized how fast and far my thoughts had carried me. I also realized my need to bring them back to their proper place.

What is that place? Isaiah 26:3 tells us. "You will keep in perfect peace all who trust in you, all whose thoughts are fixed on you!" (NLT).

We're to keep our thoughts trained, focused, glued on God. Doing so prevents them from racing down paths that leads to fear and frustration. Doing so leads to peace.

I'd choose peace over the other option any day. How about you?

Take Action: Are your thoughts fixed on God? If not, determine now to bring them back.

No Task Too Menial

Lord, grant me willingness to get my hands dirty.

I meet a lot of men and women in leadership positions. Some impress me more than others. The deciding factor? Their attitude towards menial tasks. Those who are willing to get their hands dirty, sometimes literally, usually make the greatest impact.

Christ demonstrated this attitude when He washed His disciples' feet (John 13:1-4). He was God's Son, yet He took on the role of a servant and performed a task that others regarded with disdain. And He did it voluntarily, with no expectation of receiving anything in return. How much more should we be willing to do likewise!

Opportunities to serve abound. You could…

- Wash dishes in your workplace staff room.
- Carry your neighbor's trash can from the curb to the door on garbage pickup day.
- Volunteer to work in the nursery at church.
- Serve food or wash dishes at a church potluck.
- Spring clean a senior's apartment.

Ask God to make you aware of opportunities to serve as Christ did. Go ahead, get your hands dirty, and set an example for those watching you.

Take Action: Read Philippians 2:1-11.

Safety in Numbers

Lord, alert me when Satan tries to isolate me.

Fatigue, two difficult family situations, and my husband's weeklong absence left me feeling overworked and underappreciated. I was home alone when Satan slipped in and whispered, "You're too tired to attend church tomorrow. Stay home. Sleep in."

Sly guy, eh? Satan knows that our isolation makes us easy prey, especially when we're tired or discouraged. Thankfully, my son phoned and invited me to sit with his family at the Sunday service. That, I'm sure, was a heaven-sent rescue. Worshipping the Lord with other believers helped restore my soul.

Like a wolf separating a lamb from the safety of the flock, Satan wants to isolate battle-weary believers. He did this to Elijah.

Afraid and running for his life, Elijah left his servant behind and walked a day's journey into the desert alone. There he prayed to die. Thankfully, God rescued him by sending a ministering angel (1 Kings 19:3-7).

How do you respond when you're feeling low? Remember, you'll find safety in numbers. Tell someone how you feel. Ask her to speak the truth to you and pray for you.

Take Action: Name a godly friend who would be willing to pray for you when you're discouraged.

Prosper

Lord, thank You for giving me the key to prosperity.

To prosper is to succeed and thrive. Prosperity commonly refers to finances, but it can also refer to thriving in one's personal life. Self-help books, mentoring, and coaching are big business nowadays because people yearn to prosper. They invest time, energy, and money to find the key.

God wants us to prosper too (Jeremiah 29:11). And He's already given us the key. Here it is: "Blessed is the one who does not walk in step with the wicked or stand in the way that sinners take or sit in the company of mockers, but whose delight is in the law of the LORD, and who meditates on his law day and night."

Simply put—live according to God's word. The result? "That person is like a tree planted by streams of water, which yields its fruit in season and whose leaf does not wither—whatever they do prospers" (Psalm 1:1-3).

Loving God's word and living our lives according to its instruction guarantees we will prosper. That doesn't mean life will be easy, but we'll have everything we need to thrive.

Take Action: Ask God to give you delight for His word.

God Sings

Lord, I'm eternally grateful for Your love.

My grandkidlets run to me with outstretched arms. "Grandma, Grandma!" they call. "You're here! I could hardly wait for you to come!" Their joy at seeing me chases my woes away and sets my heart to dancin'.

How much greater a response should God's love evoke in us? Zephaniah 3:17 says, "The LORD your God is with you, the Mighty Warrior who saves. He will take great delight in you; in his love he will no longer rebuke you, but will rejoice over you with singing."

Take a moment, and reread that verse. Savor every word. Close your eyes and bask in its life-changing truth.

Imagine—God is with you today. He's your mighty Savior, willing and able to fight your battles for you. He delights in you. He quiets your rush and calms your fears. He thrills over you with song.

Let this knowledge wash your worries away. Let it restore your soul, your security, and your sense of self-worth. Let it grant courage and confidence.

God loves you. May that truth set your heart to dancin' today.

Take Action: Read Zephaniah 3:17 aloud, replacing "you" with "me."

Supernatural Energy

Lord, teach me to rely on Your strength today.

Weary from the inside out—that's how we feel sometimes. Work, family, health, finances—issues with any of these things can sap our physical, mental, emotional, and spiritual energy.

How do we find renewal? Where do we find refreshment?

Isaiah 40:29-31 holds the key. "He gives strength to the weary and increases the power of the weak...Those who hope in the LORD will renew their strength. They will soar on wings like eagles; they will run and not grow weary, they will walk and not be faint."

We find renewed energy when we acknowledge God as our source of strength. We admit we need Him, we seek Him every day, and we practice His ongoing presence. Intimacy with Him restores us from the inside out.

Our strength, limited as it is, runs short quickly. But God's supply knows no end, and it's ours for the asking.

Take Action: Write Isaiah 41:10 on a recipe card. Post it where it offers a constant reminder that God is the source of your strength.

Reverence and Respect

Lord, someone's hurt me. Show me how to respond.

King Saul's relationship with David was testy at best. Saul hunted David, threw spears at him, and gave his wife to another man. He forced David into hiding and stripped him of his status as a military leader. Years of such behavior ended only when Saul died.

David might have said, "Well, well…serves you right." But he didn't. Instead, he mourned and avenged Saul's death. He said Saul was loved and admired, and he called him "the LORD's anointed." He even promised favor to those who provided a decent burial (2 Samuel 1:15–2:6).

What freed David to respect the man who had treated him so unfairly? His reverence for God and his desire to please Him. This, rather than his emotions, dictated his attitudes and actions.

When family or coworkers mistreat us, we may feel tempted to respond in kind, to give them what we think they deserve. But let's not stoop to that level. Instead, let's follow David's example—revere God, respect man.

Based on circumstances, this might sound ludicrous or impossible, but God always enables us to do what honors Him. He did it for David, and He'll do it for us.

Take Action: Pray for someone who's hurt you.

Praying Scripture

Lord, thank You for the power of Your word.

For years I prayed the same request for my family: "God, please be with them, bless them, and keep them safe." Things changed when I learned to pray Scripture.

For instance, I asked God to teach my kids to store up His commands, turn their ears to wisdom, apply their hearts to understanding, and to seek for understanding as for hidden treasure. I asked Him to bless them with a fear and knowledge of Him for doing these things (Proverbs 2:1-5). I took hold of the power in God's written word and used it to make an eternal difference.

When we pray God's word, we wield the sword of the Spirit against the enemy (Ephesians 6:17). Using phrases from Scripture is powerful because—as long as we keep them in context—they help us to pray according to God's will. And that guarantees that He hears and will answer (1 John 5:14-15).

You, too, can deepen your prayer life by incorporating God's word. Begin with the same requests I mentioned above, and then use other verses that speak to you. Your prayer life will be transformed.

Take Action: Read Psalm 1:1-3 and turn it into a prayer for your loved ones.

Completely Trustworthy

*Lord, grant me the ability to trust You
for everything that concerns me.*

On a scale of one to ten, how would you rate your ability to trust God in all things?

Scoring ten in every area of our lives is impossible for most of us. Why? We lack an accurate understanding of God's character.

Many times we view God through the distorted lens of our experiences rather than the clear lens of His word. We focus on circumstances and what-ifs rather than His promises. Big mistake.

Psalm 33:4 says, "The word of the LORD is right and true; he is faithful in all he does." The New Living Translation says, "The word of the LORD holds true, and we can trust everything he does." Everything, my friend.

Someone gave me this advice: When circumstances make you fearful, ask yourself what aspect of God's character you're not trusting. Identify it and then search the Bible for a verse that reveals the truth about that characteristic.

I pass this advice to you. Improve your understanding of God's character, and your ability to trust God will improve too.

Take Action: What aspect of God's character is most meaningful to you at this time? Why?

Immeasurable Love

Lord, thanks for loving me with
a love that can't be measured.

I love you," I tell my grandkidlets.

"How much?" they ask.

"T-h-i-s much," I say, extending my arms sideways as far as they'll reach.

All of us enjoy knowing we're loved. The most significant reminder of all time, however, came when Jesus—God in flesh—humbled Himself and descended from heaven to live among mankind. He was perfect in nature, yet He took our sin upon Himself and then bore our punishment for falling short of God's standard. He suffered humiliation and beatings, died on a cross, and was buried in a borrowed tomb…all for our sake.

"This is how God showed his love among us," says 1 John 4:9. "He sent his one and only Son into the world that we might live through him."

Sometimes we question God's love. We ask Him to provide a reminder, forgetting that He's already done so in the person of Jesus Christ.

How much does God love us? T-h-i-s much. Jesus spread His arms on the cross, and then He died for you and me.

Take Action: Spend a few moments meditating on the immensity of God's love for you.

Pure Thoughts

*Lord, teach me to fill my mind with
thoughts that honor You.*

As a young married woman, I became a huge fan of
easy-listening tunes. One day I paused and listened
to a singer croon "Torn Between Two Lovers." In that
instant, I realized I was living a double standard.

"Why am I allowing thoughts about infidelity into
my brain?" I wondered. "I value my marriage. Shouldn't
I ensure my thoughts remain pure and committed to
my husband?"

Human nature being what it is, we tend to become
what we think about most. That's why God instructs us
to discipline our minds. Philippians 4:8 says, "Finally,
brothers and sisters, whatever is true, whatever is noble,
whatever is right, whatever is pure, whatever is lovely,
whatever is admirable—if anything is excellent or
praiseworthy—think about such things."

The thoughts we habitually entertain determine
the direction of our lives. Knowing that, let's zealously
scrutinize and protect them. Let's compare them to the
standard set in Philippians 4:8. If they don't measure
up, let's ask the Holy Spirit to banish them. Let's settle
for nothing less than God's best.

Take Action: Memorize Philippians 4:8. Recite this
verse anytime inappropriate thoughts come to mind.

I Doubt It

Lord, forgive me for doubting You.

How do we feel when people who are less experienced than we are doubt our abilities? Insulted or underappreciated, right? How, then, must God feel when frail humanity doubts Him?

The Israelites learned the hard way. "They spoke against God; they said, 'Can God really spread a table in the wilderness? True, he struck the rock, and water gushed out, streams flowed abundantly, but can he also give us bread? Can he supply meat for his people?'" (Psalm 78:19-20).

Their unbelief kindled God's anger, and He responded with a mighty show of power. Unfortunately, the people refused to believe in Him or trust in His deliverance (verses 22-32).

Thankfully, we don't behave the same way. Or do we?

"God owns the universe, but can He provide for us?"

"He raises the dead, but can He protect us?"

"He designed DNA, but can He guide me?"

Fear reveals our unbelief. Imagine—the audacity of doubting the Divine.

Let's learn from the Israelites' mistake. Acknowledge unbelief as sin and give God the honor He deserves.

Take Action: With what area of unbelief do you wrestle? Confess unbelief as sin and ask God for greater faith.

Say Yes!

*Lord, please grant me the courage
to say yes unconditionally.*

Moses commissioned twelve spies to investigate the Promised Land and report their findings. Upon their return, ten of the spies focused on the problems they'd face if they invaded as God commanded. They convinced the masses to stay put and be safe.

But the other two spies, Caleb and Joshua, saw things differently. They knew God was bigger than any obstacle and urged the people to trust Him despite the risks involved.

Sadly, majority ruled. The result? God killed the ten spies, and the Israelites wandered in the wilderness for 40 years. Joshua and Caleb alone received the honor of entering the Promised Land (Numbers 13–14).

Sometimes God asks us to do something risky. This tests our faith and lands us in one of two categories—those who say no and those who say yes.

Saying no as ten of the spies did gives us the feeling of safety, but it brings spiritual consequences. Saying yes as Joshua and Caleb did requires courage and trust, but it brings blessing. Following their example seems a no-brainer, doesn't it?

Take Action: Name a situation that called for God-given risk. How did you respond? What was the result?

Be a Risk Taker

*Lord, grant me courage to say yes
to God-ordained risks.*

Esther was only a teenager when God gave her the task of saving the Jews. This involved risk, for she'd have to appear before King Xerxes uninvited. He would order her killed if he didn't welcome her presence.

Esther knew she'd fail unless God showed up. She rallied others to fast and pray, and then she moved forward, trusting God for the outcome. Scary? Yes. But watching God work through her was no doubt one of the most exciting experiences of her life (Esther 4:11-16).

Sometimes God's purposes require us to take risks. These may involve our finances, our family's comfort, our reputation, or even our safety. Our tendency might be to say no, but let's think twice.

Accepting God's invitation to participate in what He's doing, especially when it involves uncertainty, guarantees a faith-stretching experience. Scary, yes. But who wouldn't want to see God provide and equip in amazing ways?

Take Action: Hebrews 11:6 says, "Without faith it is impossible to please God." Are you living in a spiritual safety zone, where faith isn't needed? If so, invite God to take you from that zone into a faith-stretching experience, and then hang on for the ride!

Well Equipped

*Lord, thanks for giving me
everything I need for victory.*

God's power is the reason I'm doing well today," confided Danae. She'd grown up surrounded by abuse and addictions. She married at age 18, but her husband's infidelity led to divorce.

Danae ricocheted from one hurtful experience to another. Things changed when a neighbor invited her to a Bible study. Eventually she placed her faith in Christ. A godly mentor came alongside, and Danae flourished.

Some women, like Danae, overcome tremendous obstacles, and they thrive. Others are stuck in a painful past. The difference, I believe, is that some live according to 2 Peter 1:3—"His divine power has given us everything we need for a godly life through our knowledge of him who called us by his own glory and goodness."

God has given us everything we need to live victoriously—His written word, biblical teaching, godly counselors and leaders, and most of all, the Holy Spirit, who guides and empowers us.

We're well equipped to rise above defeat. We only need to utilize the gifts that are already at our disposal.

Take Action: List five gifts God has given you to empower you to live victoriously. Are you utilizing each one? If not, why not?

Invincible

Lord, thank You for making me an overcomer.

We celebrate Olympic victories, especially when athletes overcome incredible odds to win. Their stories move us, and we marvel at the sacrifices made.

Jesus followers are winners too but of a different sort. We struggle through trials. We wrestle against spiritual forces seeking to destroy us. We feel betrayed, wondering why the Divine allows the innocent to suffer while evil wins. And then we're reminded, "If God is for us, who can be against us?…In all these things we are more than conquerors through him who loved us" (Romans 8:31,37).

Satan is determined to defeat us with discouragement and lies. "Life is too hard," he hisses. "There's no hope. God has abandoned you. You're on your own."

The enemy spits his venom at us, but Almighty God loves us, indwells us, and equips us for victory (Ephesians 6:10-17).

Stand firm, my friend. Be strong in the Lord and in his mighty power. Nothing can defeat you when God is on your side. In everything you are an overcomer.

Take Action: Review Ephesians 6:10-17 every morning, starting today. Turn this passage into prayer and thank God for giving you everything you need for victory.

True Treasure

Lord, please teach me to treasure the right things.

What do you treasure most?

Each of us will answer differently. One might say, "My grandmother's heirloom china." Another, "Good health." A third, "My family." And so the list continues.

The question has no right or wrong answer, but our responses say a lot about who we are. They also dictate where we spend our energy, time, and resources. With life as short as it is, let's strive to treasure what matters most. Here's the guiding principle to determine what that means.

"Do not store up for yourselves treasures on earth... But store up for yourselves treasures in heaven, where moths and vermin do not destroy, and where thieves do not break in and steal. For where your treasure is, there your heart will be also" (Matthew 6:19-21).

These words encourage us to evaluate our priorities and keep them where they ought to be. What that looks like in practical terms varies from person to person, but the principle is universal and remains unchanged—we are to treasure most that which lasts for eternity.

Take Action: What do you treasure most? Is it of eternal value? If not, what changes can you make?

Songs at Midnight

Lord, You're worthy of all my praise.

Paul and Silas held a praise concert at midnight. And what a concert it was!

Hours prior, Paul and Silas were stripped, beaten, and thrown into a dungeon.

No doubt the men faced a sleepless night. Their cell was dark and damp. Their bodies throbbed. The stocks hurt. They knew the morning wouldn't look pretty for them. They could have panicked, but they didn't. Instead, they broke into praise. "About midnight Paul and Silas were praying and singing hymns to God, and the other prisoners were listening to them" (Acts 16:25).

An earthquake shook the prison, doors flew open, chains fell off, and people placed their faith in Jesus. Might Paul and Silas' praise have opened the door for these miracles?

Praising God in the midnight hour shows that we trust Him in the darkness, when our future looks uncertain. This response musters our faith, honors Him, and leaves a lasting impression on those watching as God powerfully works in and through us.

Let's sing, sister. When the midnight hour comes, let's sing.

Take Action: Ask God for the ability to praise in the midnight hour.

No Broken Promises

Lord, thanks for always keeping Your promises.

Chances are you've experienced a broken promise. Perhaps it happened in childhood, when a parent promised a reward for good grades. You excelled, but that reward never came. Maybe it happened in your adulthood. Someone promised, "Till death do us part," but then he left. Perhaps it happened in your workplace or even in your church.

Broken promises cause us to doubt our worth or ability. They also leave us doubting the integrity of the person who made the promise.

Thankfully, we need never doubt God's integrity because He does what He says He'll do. "It is impossible for God to lie…We have this hope as an anchor for the soul, firm and secure" (Hebrews 6:18-19).

We often assume we'll see God's promises fulfilled quickly. It's nice when that happens, but it's not guaranteed. God operates on an eternal timeline, while ours is finite. We need to trust His wisdom and His ways even when we don't understand them.

People might break their promises, but God will always keep His word. Count on it, my friend, even when the promise seems delayed.

Take Action: Read Proverbs 3:5-6. On what condition is this promise fulfilled?

My Future Is Secure

Lord, thank You for holding my future.

My youngest daughter, Kim, felt stressed as she approached high school graduation. "I wish people would stop asking about my plans for the fall," she cried. "I don't know what to do, so I don't have an answer." We prayed together nightly, thanking God in advance for guiding her steps and asking Him to give her the faith to trust Him.

Trusting God with our future can be difficult at times. We want answers to our questions. Whom will I marry? Will I have children? Will I maintain my health? What will my finances look like when I reach retirement?

We can easily grow anxious or fearful of the future, especially considering we have little or no control over it. However, knowing that God is in control brings us comfort.

Psalm 31:14-15 says, "But I trust in you, LORD; I say, 'You are my God.' My times are in your hands." The New Living Translation says, "My future is in your hands."

Are you fearful about your future? Worried because you have neither answers nor control?

Relax. Your future is secure in God's hands.

Take Action: Pray Psalm 31:14-15 aloud.

Triumph

Lord, thanks for enabling me
to triumph over life's blows.

I interviewed singer Tammy Trent several years after her husband drowned in a diving accident. She recalled suffering intense grief and loneliness, but she also affirmed that God comforted and strengthened her to face life without her soul mate. Today she shares her story nationwide.

"People need to know that whatever their challenge, they'll get through it not somehow, but triumphantly," says Tammy. "I miss my husband with every breath I take. I can't change what happened, but I can wake up today with great anticipation and expectation knowing God is always in control and up to something great. Now I wake up and say, 'What do we do today, Jesus?'"

Tammy's experience mirrors the apostle Paul's. "We are hard pressed on every side, but not crushed; perplexed, but not in despair; persecuted, but not abandoned; struck down, but not destroyed" (2 Corinthians 4:8-9).

Trials come in all shapes and sizes. No matter how large, they cannot keep us down. God's power gives us the ability to triumph. We, too, can know with certainty that God is in control and up to something great.

Take Action: Memorize 2 Corinthians 4:8-9.

Sacrifice of Thanks

Lord, please enable me to give thanks
regardless of the difficulties I face.

Max Lucado says, "God never promises to remove us from our struggles. He does promise, however, to change the way we look at them." [2]

Everyone agrees that giving thanks is easy when struggles are nonexistent, but inevitably, stuff happens. We view our struggles as inconveniences. Hassles. Heartbreaks. We see them as anything but welcome until we read and heed Psalm 50:23—"He who sacrifices thank offerings honors me, and to the blameless I will show my salvation."

Our perspective shifts when we begin giving thanks as an act of obedience in the midst of our sorrows. Doing so means we're choosing to trust God's sovereignty and purpose despite our pain, and this honors Him.

Our struggles don't disappear, but our negative attitude toward them does. It's replaced by the ability to focus on God's presence, power, and purpose. And with that comes peace.

Let's not ask God to remove our struggles from us. Rather, let's ask Him to change our view of them, and let's cooperate by offering sacrifices of thanks.

Take Action: Express gratitude for three things in your current or recent struggle.

Precious Offerings

Lord, help me to offer You thanksgiving
even when life hurts.

Attendees at a coaching seminar were told to give a treasured belonging to a classmate. A young man presented his offering to me—a silver dollar.

"My grandfather gave this coin to me when I was ten years old," he said. "As an adult, I've always kept it on my desk as a visual reminder of his influence on my life."

I scarcely knew how to respond. This coin was a sacrificial gift. Receiving it made me feel honored.

Scripture tells us to present sacrificial offerings to God. One of the most meaningful offerings we can give Him is thanksgiving in the midst of life's difficulties. "Sacrifice thank offerings to God, fulfill your vows to the Most High, and call upon me in the day of trouble; I will deliver you, and you will honor me," says Psalm 50:14-15.

Thanking God for His faithfulness and love in the midst of trials shows we trust Him even when we hurt. What a gift! Sacrificial, yes, but it honors Him. And it's one we can give many times throughout our lives, beginning today.

Take Action: Identify a challenge you face and pray, "Father, I thank You for _____."

Morning Song

Lord, start my day with a song.

What's the first thing on your mind when you wake—your to-do list? A difficult relationship? An upsetting conversation?

Our waking moments play a significant role in our day's direction. Waking to angry, fearful, or critical thoughts promises a not-so-good day. Waking with praise and thanksgiving guarantees the opposite.

I set my alarm to a local Christian radio station. This fills my waking moments with worship songs. They fix my mind on Christ rather than the clutter clamoring for my attention.

Psalm 59:16 says, "I will sing of your strength, in the morning I will sing of your love; for you are my fortress, my refuge in times of trouble."

Meditate on such truths before rolling out of bed to begin the day. Doing so equips us to respond to rather than react to petty annoyances. We'll display courage in the face of storms, and we'll learn to rest quietly in God's love.

The effect of starting each day with praise might astound us. Let's make it a daily discipline and see what changes occur.

Take Action: Memorize Psalm 59:16-17 and recite it each morning as you begin your day.

Defeat Defeat

*Lord, thank You for deleting
the word "defeat" from my vocabulary.*

By all appearances, David was defeated. He'd joined the Philistines to fight against Israel, but someone questioned his integrity and sent him home. When he and his men arrived at their city, however, they found it destroyed and their wives and children taken captive. As if that weren't enough, David's army then plotted to stone him (1 Samuel 29:9-11; 30:1-6).

David appeared defeated, but he refused to quit. Instead, "David found strength in the LORD his God" and launched a major offensive to retrieve the captives and stolen possessions (30:7-8).

Difficult circumstances can sometimes leave us feeling defeated, but we needn't succumb. Like David, we can find strength in God. What does that look like?

We admit our weakness and dependence upon Him. We focus on His promises. We practice praise. And we rally other believers to pray for us.

With God on our side, we have everything necessary to defeat defeat, and victory is ours.

Take Action: Memorize Psalm 118:13-14—"I was pushed back and about to fall, but the Lord helped me. The Lord is my strength and my defense; he has become my salvation."

My Weakness, God's Strength

Lord, I praise You for being the strong one.

Kelita Haverland is a Canadian singer and comedienne whose life has been touched by divorce, suicide, infidelity, abortion, and more.

"My attitude for years was, 'I'm strong; I'll rise above whatever is thrown my way,'" says Kelita. "But I did it on my own, never asking God for help. The weight of doing so exhausted me, and my health broke down."

Kelita found freedom in God's word: "'My grace is all you need. My power works best in weakness.' So now I am glad to boast about my weaknesses, so that that the power of Christ can work through me...For when I am weak, then I am strong" (2 Corinthians 12:9-10 NLT). Her message resonates with many.

We ask each other, "How are you?" and we answer, "Fine." Our self-sufficiency masks our fear of inadequacy and rejection. Stress increases, and our well-being suffers. But God has a better way.

Let's admit our need for help. We don't have to be the strong ones. He's the strong one, and His power is perfected in our weakness.

Take Action: Are you trying to overcome hurts in your own strength? Admit your weakness and ask God for His strength.

Making Plans

*Lord, help me keep You foremost
in my decision making.*

My husband and I built our dream house. More accurately, an architect translated our ideas into blueprints, and a team of skilled laborers constructed it.

These men possessed skill and knowledge we lacked. Employing them resulted in a lovely home that satisfied building codes. Imagine the fiasco if we'd attempted the project without seeking the experts!

Sounds a lot like life, doesn't it? Before we try to convert our dreams and plans into reality, we need to seek the Master Builder. God's word instructs us to commit our ideas to the Lord, to submit them to His expertise. "Commit everything you do to the LORD. Trust him, and he will help you" (Psalm 37:5 NLT).

We can create a fiasco if we plunge headlong into our plans without first consulting the Expert and giving Him the freedom to do with them whatever He knows is best. Let's save ourselves trouble by inviting His involvement from the get-go.

Take Action: What dreams are in your heart? Commit them to God today.

The Spirit Prays

Lord, I'm so grateful You know what to pray at all times.

Women often email me with their stories. One lady recently wrote about her son, a drug addict serving time for robbery. Another wrote of trying to mend her marriage following her husband's infidelity. Numerous others have shared about infertility, miscarriages, abuse, and divorce.

I read their stories and yearn to fix their situations. Remove their pain. Restore their joy.

Unfortunately, I can't do any of that. But I can pray.

Sometimes words come easily; other times not. Needs are so massive that I scarcely know where to begin. That's when Romans 8:26-27 comforts me. "The Spirit helps us in our weakness. We do not know what we ought to pray for, but the Spirit himself intercedes for us through wordless groans...The Spirit intercedes for God's people in accordance with the will of God."

Perhaps words fail you at times too. Take comfort in knowing that God understands your heart's cry. The Spirit intercedes on your behalf when you don't know what to pray.

Take Action: What situation leaves you at a loss regarding what to pray? Thank the Holy Spirit for praying for you.

Impossible? No.

Lord, I praise You for being God of the impossible.

"Nothing is impossible with God." An angel spoke these words to a virgin teenager after saying she would conceive and give birth to God's Son. Then he added that the teen's elderly and barren relative, Elizabeth, was pregnant and would deliver a child in three months (Luke 1:35-37 NLT).

The angel's words came true. God does what people say cannot be done. Performing the impossible is nothing for Him.

What seemingly impossible situation are you facing? You see no way around it, no way out, and no way through. But the Holy Spirit whispers, "Don't give up. Your desire will come to pass, for nothing is impossible with God." His quiet voice says, "Don't lose hope. This situation seems impossible, but doing the impossible is nothing for God."

Whatever impossibility you are facing, remember the teenager Mary. Recall her cousin Elizabeth. Remember the odds stacked against them. And know that those odds mean nothing in light of the angel's declaration.

Take Action: Name the impossibility you face. Is it a too-heavy workload? A family or financial crisis? An impending deadline? Praise God that nothing is impossible for Him, and refuse to be discouraged.

In His Arms

Lord, thank You for carrying me in Your arms.

My son, Matthew, has five young children. Watching him interact with them warms my heart. I'm especially touched when I see him carry them.

He shoulders them when they're tired or they need an unobstructed view. He wraps them in his arms when they feel afraid. And he cradles them while they sleep.

Earthly fathers are meant to mirror the heavenly Father, and Matt performs his role well. He especially reflects Psalm 68:19—"Praise the Lord; praise God our savior! For each day he carries us in his arms" (NLT).

Our heavenly Father loves us dearly. He provides for us, teaches us, and disciplines us. And He carries us in His arms.

He shoulders us when life saps our strength and we feel too weary to walk.

He lifts us up and gives us a new perspective when our view of life is obstructed.

He wraps us in His arms and comforts us when we feel afraid.

Our Father's arms provide strength, solace, and security, and they're always open. Run to them and nestle there today!

Take Action: How do you envision God carrying you? Draw a picture of yourself in His arms.

An In-Tune Heart

Lord, keep my heart tuned to Yours.

The school band was rehearsing a song prior to the year-end concert. "Stop!" said the conductor.

He pointed at a saxophonist. "Fix it." The sax player made a small tweak, and the rehearsal resumed.

To be most effective in their art, musicians must keep their instruments in tune. The principle holds true in the spiritual realm. Believers must keep their hearts in tune to be most effective in their role as kingdom builders.

Psalm 125:4 says, "O LORD, do good to those who are good, whose hearts are in tune with you" NLT. What are some of the characteristics of a heart that's in tune with God?

- It values what God values.
- It recognizes divine appointments.
- It grieves over things that grieve God.
- It refuses to let fear hinder obedience.
- It practices the art of thanksgiving in any situation.

Let's ask the Holy Spirit to show us where we need to make an adjustment, and then let's do what He says.

Take Action: How can you ensure your heart remains in tune with God?

Masterpiece

Lord, thanks for making me Your masterpiece.

A Polish girlfriend recently gave me a handmade gift. Using an empty wine bottle, paint, decoupage, and paper napkins, she created a masterpiece featuring yellow sunflowers against a lime-green background.

The decorative bottle reminds me of my friend. It also reminds me of the truth found in Philippians 1:6— "He who began a good work in you will carry it on to completion until the day of Christ Jesus."

God works constantly in our lives. He uses the mundane and the extraordinary to shape us. He uses tragedy and triumph to refine us.

Sometimes we protest the Divine Designer's methods, thinking we know better. Thankfully, He doesn't give up and walk away, leaving His work half-done. Instead, He patiently continues His labor of love because He's promised to complete the good work He has begun in us.

Whatever your day holds, remember—you're a masterpiece in the making. God is creating a woman of strength and beauty, filled and controlled by His Spirit. Let Him have His way.

Take Action: Ask God to use this day's events to make you more like a finished masterpiece.

Hope amid Failure

*Lord, thanks for offering hope and
restoration when I fail You.*

A woman called me recently. "I had an affair several years ago," she said. "My husband has forgiven me, and we're doing relatively well. I know God has forgiven me too, but I keep beating myself up for what happened. Help me! I'm stuck."

Many of us can relate. Past failures keep us mired in regret, and we feel powerless to change.

There's good news! Jesus knew about our failure even before it occurred, and He prayed on our behalf. Note His interaction with Simon Peter prior to his denial of Him: "But I have pleaded in prayer for you, Simon, that your faith should not fail. So when you have repented and turned to me again, strengthen your brothers" (Luke 22:32 NLT).

Even before our failure, Jesus prayed that our faith would not fail as a result. He was pleading for our repentance and restoration. And now He encourages us to move forward and strengthen others who are struggling.

Past failures needn't spell defeat—especially when Jesus Himself has been praying on our behalf.

Take Action: Read Luke 22:32 aloud. Replace Simon's name with yours.

Give Yourself a Gift

*Lord, please enable me to forgive those
who have hurt me.*

Forgiveness is a God-given gift, but it's also a gift we give ourselves. Yet sometimes we hesitate to offer it. Perhaps that's because we misunderstand what it really is.

Some folks mistakenly think forgiving their offender means putting a stamp of approval on the offense. Some think it means letting the offender off the hook. These are misperceptions.

Forgiveness is a process by which we choose to do what's right by God's standard. "As God's chosen people, holy and dearly loved…Forgive one another if any of you has a grievance against someone. Forgive as the Lord forgave you" (Colossians 3:12-13).

Forgiveness has nothing to do with the offender. It's about obedience on our part. When we obey, God blesses us by setting us free from the past and empowering us to embrace the future. Therefore, forgiveness is a gift we give ourselves.

If someone has hurt you, do what's right. Give yourself a gift by forgiving your offender.

Take Action: Ask God to help you see your offender through His eyes.

When Thoughts Differ

*Lord, help me rest when
I don't understand Your thoughts.*

Gene and I had worked at a Christian camp for nine years when cancer claimed the general director's life. The board sought to fill his position, so Gene applied. He seemed the logical replacement.

Shock and disappointment hit us when the board chose someone else, but we chose to trust during that difficult time. Isaiah 55:8-9 became a mainstay—"'My thoughts are not your thoughts, neither are your ways my ways,' declares the LORD. 'As the heavens are higher than the earth, so are my ways higher than your ways and my thoughts than your thoughts.'"

Nine months later, a US-based ministry asked us to launch a Canadian office. Our main role was to lead volunteer teams to host evangelistic summer family camps in Eastern Europe. Using our camping experience to grow an international ministry had never crossed our minds.

Sometimes God's thoughts baffle us. We question, cry, and wrestle. And yet the truth remains—He knows best. At all times. May we learn to trust Him and rest even when His thoughts and ours don't align.

Take Action: What God-thoughts don't you understand? Ask Him for faith to trust.

Expect More

Lord, teach me to expect more of You.

Peter was in chains and guarded by 16 soldiers. Escape was unthinkable, "but the church was earnestly praying to God for him" (Acts 12:5).

God's answer astounded everyone. An angel arrived, chains fell off, Peter walked past guards unnoticed, and prison gates opened before him. He went to the house where the church was praying, and he knocked on the door.

The sound of Peter's voice so shocked the servant that she forgot to let him in. She ran to tell the crowd that God had answered their prayers, but they thought she'd gone crazy. When they finally saw Peter standing there, they were astonished (verses 6-17).

O ye of little faith.

O *we* of little faith.

Do you suppose we expect too little in prayer? God says He is "able to do immeasurably more than all we ask or imagine" (Ephesians 3:20). Do we believe Him? If so, perhaps we ought to think bigger and trust Him for mind-boggling answers.

For what are you trusting God today? Ask Him to astound you with the answer.

Take Action: Ask a friend to pray and believe with you for God to answer your prayer in an amazing way.

Trained for Battle

Lord, remind me to utilize the battle gear
You've provided.

The Scriptures are clear—believers are engaged in a spiritual battle. The Bible tells us to wear the armor of God to withstand the devil's schemes, and then it gives a detailed description about what that armor entails (Ephesians 6:10-18). No doubt God has adequately equipped us to fight the enemy.

But sometimes we don't feel equipped. We forget that the Holy Spirit, who dwells within us, is the same Spirit whose power raised Christ from the dead. We allow our circumstances to overwhelm us. We wave the white flag of surrender and succumb to defeat.

That's not the destiny God intends for us!

Fighting a spiritual battle can be dangerous and disheartening, but "defeat" should never be in our vocabulary. "Praise be to the LORD my Rock, who trains my hands for war, my fingers for battle. He is my loving God and my fortress, my stronghold and my deliverer, my shield, in whom I take refuge, who subdues peoples under me," says Psalm 144:1-2.

What battle are you waging today? Remember, God has equipped you to fight. With Him on your side, victory is sure.

Take Action: Read Psalm 18:32-40.

Count It Pure Joy

Lord, help me respond well to trials.

My left Achilles tendon ruptured during the writing of this book. Nine days later, my right knee blew. My go, go, go nature slammed to an immediate halt, and I learned the reality of James 1:2-4—"When troubles come your way, consider it an opportunity for great joy. For you know that when your faith is tested, your endurance has a chance to grow. So let it grow, for when your endurance is fully developed, you will be perfect and complete, needing nothing" (NLT).

Learning to ask others for help became an opportunity for joy. So did calf cramps, crutches, canceling a trip to Moscow, and pulling myself up three flights of stairs on my behind to reach my bedroom every night. I shed a few tears, but God's promise to strengthen my character and equip me for anything gave me hope.

Troubles can be our friends when we remember God's purpose for allowing them in our lives. Don't waste or fight them. Embrace them as personal and spiritual growth opportunities. The end result—strong character—is worth it.

Take Action: Are you facing a trial today? Fill in the blank: "I will consider _____ pure joy."

Panic or Peace?

Lord, thank You for reigning over life's storms.

My husband loves to sail. He touts, "The stormier the weather, the better!" I can't relate to his perspective, but I can relate to the disciples' terror when a storm sent waves crashing over their boat. If I'd been there, I'd have joined their panic: "Lord, save us! We're going to drown!" (Matthew 8:24).

I would also have seen the sleeping Jesus—peace personified—wake to challenge the disciples not to fear and then command the storm to cease.

Life's storms, like the weather-related storms in this biblical account, often strike when least expected, and our natural response is to fear. Maybe our perspective needs a shift.

Perhaps we ought to consider storms as opportunities to experience God in new ways. When fearful circumstances threaten to reign over us, let's ask Christ to reign over our circumstances. Let's invite Him to prove His promises and increase our faith.

No doubt He will answer, and we'll learn to rest in the storms.

Take Action: Panic or peace? Which one best describes your response in life's storms? What changes can you make so you can rest in the storms?

Everything We Need

Lord, help me remember I have everything I need for godly living.

Physical life being what it is, we need to replenish consumable goods. We eat groceries, outgrow clothes, wear out shoes, and deplete cleaning supplies. We often keep a list of goods we buy on a weekly basis. Seems there's always something.

The opposite is true for our spiritual lives: "By his divine power, God has given us everything we need for living a godly life. We have received all of this by coming to know him, the one who called us to himself by means of his marvelous glory and excellence! And because of his glory and excellence, he has given us great and precious promises" (2 Peter 1:3-4 NLT).

God's power never runs out. By it we have everything necessary to live victorious, godly lives. Christ living in us enables us to forgive our enemies, resist temptation, rise above fear, rejoice always, and more.

Defeat comes not because we lack resources, but because we don't appropriate those resources, including God's word, prayer, and the Holy Spirit's power.

As believers, we possess everything we need to live godly lives. How does this truth affect your life today?

Take Action: Feeling defeated? Thank God for supplying everything you need for victory.

True Heroes

Lord, thanks for godly examples You've put in my life.

My grandson Luke finds superheroes fascinating. One day he said, "When I sneeze, fire comes out my pockets and I run really fast." He gave a mock *achoo* and raced through my kitchen and living room.

Our society hails heroes as those who perform extraordinary acts of courage, but what about the unsung heroes who...

- guard the dignity of seniors and people with special needs
- open their homes for abused or abandoned children
- spend hours in intercessory prayer
- suffer with chronic pain or terminal illness without complaint
- sacrifice comfort or safety to follow God's call

The psalmist wrote, "The godly people in the land are my true heroes! I take pleasure in them!" (Psalm 16:3 NLT). Let's celebrate those who perform extraordinary acts of courage, but let's also applaud those who demonstrate God's heart, values, and character despite personal sacrifice or discouraging circumstances.

Take Action: Who's a hero to you? Encourage that person today with an email or phone call.

A Relevant Savior

Lord, thank You for loving me as I am.

Jesus encountered people of every sort, including tax collectors, criminals, grief-stricken parents, lepers, beggars, prostitutes, naked demoniacs, and fishermen. Men and women—messy, proud, sick, and broken—approached Him. Not once did He say, "Stand back. Take a shower and clean up your act. Then I'll talk with you."

Jesus accepted people where they were. He stooped to listen. He extended His hand. He healed them. Relationship began—"I will be their God, and they will be my people" (Hebrews 8:10)—and transformation followed.

How blessed we are to know that Jesus accepts us where we are. Sinners by nature, we'd be without hope if He expected us to measure up to His standard of holiness before He welcomed and loved us.

Do we, as His followers, reflect His heart to others? Do we accept the messy and the broken where they are, or do we withhold relationship until they become what others think they ought to be? We're never to stamp our approval on sinful behavior, but we're to love people because God values them.

Jesus did this. Do we?

Take Action: Ask God to help you see hurting and broken people through His eyes.

The Real Enemy

Lord, please make me mindful of who the real enemy is.

Life would be so easy if it weren't for people! The human race seems to be notorious for complicating everything. Family feuds, adultery, abuse, cheating, lying—none of the mess caused by these things would happen if it weren't for people, right?

Wrong.

In the past I felt frustration or anger when others hurt me. In some cases, I even mentally categorized offenders as my enemies. Sure, I'd pray for them because the Bible said I should, but still, loving them was tough.

My heart changed as I pondered Paul's words to the Ephesians: "Our struggle is not against flesh and blood, but against the rulers, against the authorities, against the powers of this dark world and against the spiritual forces of evil in the heavenly realms" (Ephesians 6:12).

People might hurt you, but they aren't your enemies. Satan is your real enemy, and his evil influence prompts hurtful people to do what they do. As Scripture says, pray for them. Love them and ask God to set them free from the enemy's grip.

Take Action: Memorize Ephesians 6:12. Recall it when someone hurts you.

He Holds You

Lord, thanks for being my security.

We recently visited relatives who'd just acquired a new dog. The pup was good natured, but she frightened our two-year-old grandson, Caleb.

On one occasion Caleb ran to me, grabbed my hand, and pressed himself against my leg. My nearness made him feel safe.

The scene illustrated Psalm 63:7-8—"Because you are my help, I sing in the shadow of your wings. I cling to you; your right hand upholds me."

Perhaps you relate to Caleb. Something is making you anxious or afraid. Maybe a loved one is in trouble. Perhaps your marriage is struggling. Maybe you've experienced major change recently—marriage, divorce, widowhood, a new child, an empty nest, a relocation, a promotion, a layoff, a new job.

God cares about your feelings. He wants to help you, to hide you in the shadow of His wings. He invites you to cling to Him, and He promises to hold you securely.

Go ahead—tell Him how you feel. Stay immersed in the Scriptures. And find a godly friend to pray with you.

Stay close to God, and everything will be all right.

Take Action: Is anything hindering you from closeness with God? If so, what is it? What changes can you make?

Two Valuable Characteristics

*Lord, make me a woman known for
loyalty and kindness.*

What character qualities matter most? Proverbs 3:3
(NLT) mentions two we can't do without. "Never
let loyalty and kindness leave you! Tie them around your
neck as a reminder. Write them deep within your heart."

People of all ages, cultures, and beliefs consider loyalty and kindness to be valuable characteristics. And
it's no wonder—healthy relationships are impossible
without them. We might be hardworking, creative, and
organized, but our people skills lack if those qualities
aren't accompanied by loyalty and kindness.

Besides that, a person who displays these will likely
possess other good qualities as well. For instance, a
woman who's loyal will be trustworthy, honest, and faithful. Someone who's kind will be loving, compassionate,
and focused on others. She'll likely be a good listener too.
Sounds like the ideal employee, neighbor, or friend.

Develop these two qualities, says Proverbs. Embed
them internally and display them externally. The result
is worth the effort, for here's what you'll receive in return:
"Then you will find favor with both God and people, and
you will earn a good reputation" (verse 4 NLT).

Take Action: List your positive character qualities. Do
they include loyalty and kindness?

For God's Glory

Lord, be glorified in all I do.

What guiding principle do you follow for making decisions?

Some women might say, "I make choices that help me get what I want." Others might say, "I choose whatever feels right at the time" or "whatever makes most sense."

Guidelines based on emotions or selfish gain cause us to make decisions we later regret, but here's a principle that provides a higher standard: "Whether you eat or drink, or whatever you do, do it all for the glory of God" (1 Corinthians 10:31 NLT).

"All" includes the clothes we wear, the conversations we hold, the online sites we visit, the television shows we watch, the relationships in which we engage, and the thoughts we entertain. It includes the things on which we spend our money and the manner in which we spend our spare time. "All" applies to every facet of our lives.

Doing all for God's glory guarantees we will make wise decisions. Make this your guiding principle, and you'll live without regret.

Take Action: Is any area of your life not glorifying God? What needs to change?

Doing a Great Work

Lord, keep me focused on the job You've given me to do.

What's your God-given role during this season of your life? Whatever it is, consider it a great work.

Follow Nehemiah's example as he rebuilt the wall around Jerusalem. When the opposition tried to lure him away, he replied, "I am carrying on a great project and cannot go down. Why should the work stop while I leave it and go down to you?" (Nehemiah 6:3).

Nehemiah's enemies tried this tactic four times, but he believed in the importance of his task and refused to abandon it.

Voices might say your work has no value and you're wasting your potential. You may be weary, feeling overworked and underappreciated.

Refuse to compare yourself with other women, especially those whose roles bring better pay and public recognition. Doing so leads to envy, frustration, or worse—leaving your great work to take on one that isn't God's choice for you.

If God has planted you in this role, it's exactly what you should be doing. Thank Him for entrusting you with this great work and ask Him to use you for His highest purposes.

Take Action: Ask God for His perspective about your role.

Helping the Poor

Lord, please give me compassion for the poor.

I hadn't seen poverty until we moved to Nepal. Our neighbors owned cooking pots and utensils, grass sleeping mats, and a few tattered clothes. Some owned fields and a water buffalo or two. But then there were others, like the mother with eight children.

Her husband had abandoned her, leaving her destitute. She came to me one day, seeking help for her youngest child—a malnourished toddler. She had a second request. "The rats are eating our rice. I need a tin can with a lid for storage."

You and I are blessed in so many ways. We are responsible to use our abundance to help others who cannot help themselves. Globally, we can sponsor kids through nonprofits that provide education, medical care, and employment. Locally, we can donate to food banks and homeless shelters. Options are endless.

Most of the world lives in poverty. We don't. Let's embrace God's values and model Proverbs 31:20— "She opens her arms to the poor and extends her hands to the needy" (NLT).

Take Action: Determine one thing you can do today to help someone less fortunate.

Follow the Leader

Lord, teach me to trust You as my leader.

A group of kids played follow the leader. Trouble was, everyone wanted that position. Finally the girl in front yelled, "I'm the leader! I can't do my job if you don't listen!" Wee wisdom.

As believers, we're to follow the Leader—our Lord. He's more than capable of fulfilling His role with excellence. "The LORD is good and does what is right; he shows the proper path to those who go astray. He leads the humble in doing right, teaching them his way. The LORD leads with unfailing love and faithfulness all who keep his covenant and obey his demands" (Psalm 25:8-10 NLT).

Everything would be okay if we would trust His lead, but sometimes we think we know better. We take a different path or rush ahead of Him. And then we wonder why we land in trouble.

The Lord's role is to lead us. Our role is to follow with a teachable spirit. We can trust Him because He leads from a heart of love for us, not from a desire for domination over us.

Are you following well?

Take Action: Read and memorize Psalm 32:8.

God's No

Lord, thanks for not giving me everything I want.

"Can you imagine the outcome if a parent honored each request of each child during a trip? We'd inch our bloated bellies from one ice-cream store to the next," writes Max Lucado.[3]

Sometimes a parent has to say no. So does God when His kids bring their requests to Him.

You'd think we'd trust His judgment, and yet we cajole. We plead. Sometimes we cry, just like the kids. We want what we want, and we want our heavenly Father to want it for us too. After all, we reason, He loves us. Shouldn't He then honor our request?

It's true—He *does* love us. But He's also wise. And that's why He says no sometimes. I shudder to think where I'd be today if He'd said yes to all the requests I thought were reasonable at the time.

"His wisdom is profound, his power is vast. Who has resisted him and come out unscathed?" (Job 9:4). Our Father declines some of our requests for a reason. Let's trust His decision and thank Him for saving us from ourselves.

Take Action: Recall an instance when God's "no" turned out for your good.

The Fear of God

Lord, teach me what fearing You really means.

I often prayed this simple prayer during my kids' formative years: "Father, teach my children to fear You." I believed that all crucial life issues would fall into place if they possessed a proper reverence for God.

For example, with an appropriate fear of God, they would seek His will for their life callings. They would marry godly spouses, establish Christ-centered homes, and raise their children to love Jesus. Reverence for God would prompt them to practice forgiveness, give thanks in all things, and live with integrity. The ramifications were endless.

Scripture teems with insights about the fear of the Lord. One nugget is found in Proverbs 9:10-11— "The fear of the LORD is the beginning of wisdom, and knowledge of the Holy One is understanding. For through wisdom your days will be many, and years will be added to your life."

Imagine how your loved ones would benefit if you asked God to give them a healthy fear of Himself. And imagine the impact on society.

Take Action: Begin praying today that your loved ones will possess a healthy fear of God.

A Wise Woman

Lord, please make me a home builder.

Pssst. Come here, Jacob," whispered Rebekah. "Your dad plans to give his blessing to your brother today. But I know how you can receive it instead." Then she unveiled a tragic plot that destroyed her twin sons' relationship (Genesis 27).

"The wise woman builds her house, but with her own hands the foolish one tears hers down," says Proverbs 14:1. Rebekah's actions tore down her household. We tsk-tsk her, but we do the same when we…

- show favoritism to certain family members
- demand perfectionism from others
- practice codependent behavior
- neglect to express love with our words or deeds
- vent our frustrations on our loved ones

Now reread the list but add the word "don't" at the start of each phrase. Once you've done this, you'll have five strategies to help build your house.

Wise is the woman who builds her house. Doing so requires intentionality, but the result is worth the effort as relationships are strengthened rather than destroyed.

Take Action: Identify one way you can build your house today and then do it.

Opportunity

*Lord, please help me recognize
opportunities You bring my way.*

Opportunities knock on our doors every day. Some are wonderful and welcome. We land a longed-for job promotion, receive an invitation to meet someone we've admired from a distance, or travel somewhere we've only dreamed of going—courtesy of another's generosity.

Other opportunities come wearing a disguise. We see them first as challenges or tragedies, but a closer look reveals unexpected treasure.

- The death of a loved one becomes an opportunity to experience God's faithfulness and comfort.

- A friend's cancer diagnosis becomes an opportunity to listen to her, encourage her, and support her.

- A child's poor choices become opportunities to pray with other moms in the same situation.

Opportunities wear different faces. Whether good or not-so-good, let's make the most of them as Ephesians 5:15 says. "Be very careful, then, how you live—not as unwise but as wise, making the most of every opportunity, because the days are evil."

Take Action: Ask the Lord to help you see your current challenge as an opportunity to learn more about His character.

Guard Your Heart

Lord, teach me to guard my heart
and keep it wholly Yours.

Guard your heart above all else, for it determines the course of your life," says Proverbs 4:23 (NLT). "Heart" is the word we use for our feelings of love and desire. We do well to protect those feelings because they impact the direction our lives take.

An unguarded heart sets no hedges or boundaries to protect itself from harm or evil. It allows itself to be tempted with things that steal its affection from the Lord. The fallout is always negative, impacting our relationships, our health, and even our finances.

Thankfully, God's mercy offers hope and restoration. But we're better off guarding our hearts proactively than having to learn the hard way. This requires setting standards of holiness that refuse entry to anything offensive to God. It also requires keeping our affections on God first and foremost.

God created us with emotions. Our feelings of love and desire are gifts. Let's cherish and protect them, knowing their power in our lives.

Take Action: Identify any unrestrained desires in your life. Ask God to take control over them.

The Gift of Friendship

Lord, thank You for the friends You've given me.

Deep woman-to-woman friendships are precious gifts, especially in our transient and busy society. Making the effort to develop them results in mutual strength and encouragement—things we can all use.

I meet monthly with two other women involved in career ministry. We spend two or three hours together, catching up on what's happened since we met last. Everything's confidential, so we share honestly from our hearts. We listen, laugh, ask questions, and sometimes cry.

Then comes the highlight—prayer. One by one, we intercede on each other's behalf for our ministries, marriages, and families. Knowing the others understand, accept, and love us leaves us refreshed, encouraged, and strengthened.

Ecclesiastes 4:9-12 speaks of the benefits of friendship. Verse 12 sums it up: "Though one may be overpowered, two can defend themselves. A cord of three strands is not quickly broken."

God created us to flourish in relationships. As women, we need each other so we can thrive through thick and thin. A friendship is a gift—let's exchange, open, and enjoy it.

Take Action: Are you enjoying a soul-friendship? If not, what needs to change?

Washing Feet

Lord, grant me a servant's heart like Yours.

Jesus modeled the essence of servanthood a few hours before He died when He poured water into a basin and washed His disciples' dust-encrusted feet (John 13:1-17). This was a nasty task they would never have undertaken—a task normally relegated to household slaves. But Jesus didn't hesitate to perform this duty, nor did He refrain from washing the feet of Judas, the one He knew would betray Him shortly.

Task complete, Jesus issued the challenge: "I have set you an example that you should do as I have done for you" (verse 15).

Marian Wright Edelman said, "Service is the rent we pay to be living. It is the very purpose of life and not something you do in your spare time."

Servanthood is not an occasional kind act, favor repaid, or expected duty done. It's the overflow of a humble heart. It's the outworking of Jesus living in us. It's to be our way of life, not something we do in our spare time.

May God grant us the ability to serve others as selflessly as Jesus did.

Take Action: Think of someone who's difficult for you to love. How can you serve that person?

Bid Anxiety Goodbye

Lord, thanks for supplying a cure for anxiety.

Anxiety weighs down the heart (Proverbs 12:25), but God has given us the cure. "Do not be anxious about anything, but in everything, by prayer and petition, with thanksgiving, present your requests to God" (Philippians 4:6).

Note that the remedy for anxiety is twofold. If you're like me, you're well acquainted with the first part—prayer and petition.

How familiar are you with the second part—thanksgiving? It's easy to whiz past it as we read about prayers, petitions, and presenting our requests to God. But there it is—give thanks.

Years ago, I began adding a postscript to my prayers: "Thank You in advance for what You're going to do." This simple sentence declared my trust in God's ability to answer, and it strengthened my faith.

The cure for anxiety is simple, but we must exercise both parts—prayer and thanks. As a result, "the peace of God, which transcends all understanding, will guard your hearts and your minds in Christ Jesus" (verse 7).

Take Action: Memorize Philippians 4:6-7.

Restraint

*Lord, help me to know when to speak
and when to keep silent.*

Television, tabloids, and social media have kissed verbal restraint goodbye. Blurting too much information with too little thought seems the accepted way. But it's not the best way. Practicing restraint in our comments and conversation always works in our favor.

Sometimes the content must be filtered to be appropriate for the audience. Sometimes the timing of our words must be carefully calculated. And sometimes we need to simply keep silent.

The latter is especially true when someone shares a confidence with us. Unless it involves illegal or harmful activity, we do well to respect that person's privacy just as we'd appreciate their doing the same for us.

Restraint is also appropriate when God plants a dream or desire in our hearts. Like Mary at Jesus' birth, we'd do well to ponder rather than immediately publicize the things God has revealed.

"Those who are trustworthy can keep a confidence," says Proverbs 11:13 (NLT). Prove yourself trustworthy by practicing verbal restraint.

Take Action: Ask the Holy Spirit to put a guard over your lips.

He's Coming

Lord, I look forward to the day You return.

It was Friday, the day my brother-in-law said he'd come to visit.

"What time will Bill arrive?" I asked my husband. "Will he be here for supper?"

"He hadn't decided when I last spoke with him," Gene replied.

Not knowing when to expect our guest, I spent the morning cleaning the house and preparing a nice meal. Doing these things early in the day meant we could welcome Bill and enjoy our visit when he arrived.

We take care to prepare for houseguests. Do we prepare as thoroughly for Christ's second coming? Scripture says His arrival is certain, but it doesn't reveal the day or time. "You also must be ready, because the Son of Man will come at an hour when you do not expect him" (Luke 12:40).

Let's be ready. Let's walk in right relationship with God—and as far as we're able, with our fellow man—on a moment-by-moment basis. Doing so ensures that we'll be able to welcome Christ when He arrives.

Take Action: What would you change about your life if you knew Christ's arrival was today?

Remember

Lord, help me to recall blessings I've received and lessons I've learned.

Moms often tell their kids to remember this and that because they're concerned for their offspring's well-being.

Our heavenly Father says "remember" to His kids too, and for the same reason. He told the Israelites, "Remember how the LORD your God led you all the way in the wilderness these forty years" (Deuteronomy 8:2)...how He supplied manna and water, how their clothes and shoes didn't wear out, and how their feet didn't swell as they walked in the desert.

God knew His kids' tendency to forget Him and thereby run into serious trouble. "If you ever forget the LORD your God and follow other gods...you will surely be destroyed" (verse 19). He wanted to spare them unnecessary heartache—thus the reminder to remember Him.

We, too, do well to remember God. Recalling times when we've experienced His presence and power instills courage in us and in others. It also produces gratitude for His blessings. Rehearsing His past works prepares us for the present and the future.

Remember God. It's for your own good.

Take Action: Recall an incident when you experienced God's faithfulness. Tell someone your story.

Prayer and Motives

Lord, please help me pray with right motives.

Shalene and Twila prayed together weekly for nearly a year. "I don't understand," said Twila one evening. "For months we've asked God to give my husband a promotion, but nothing has happened. What's with that?"

"Perhaps our motives aren't right," said Shalene.

"What do you mean?"

"Be honest. What's the reason for wanting a promotion? Do you really need the income, or do you just want the stuff extra income can buy?"

Twila stared out the window for a few moments. Finally she broke the silence. "You would ask that. You're right—this has been all about my wants, not what's best for my husband or family. No wonder God hasn't said yes."

Motives matter to God. He knows what's in our hearts, and He responds accordingly. Selfish motives get nowhere with Him. "When you ask, you do not receive, because you ask with wrong motives, that you may spend what you get on your pleasures" (James 4:3).

Do you want an effective prayer life? Let's invite God to examine our motives and ensure they're pure so our requests won't be hindered.

Take Action: Do it—ask God to examine your motives.

Christ in Me

Lord, I'm amazed that You live in me.

Believers have every reason to face life with courage and confidence. The apostle Paul demonstrates why—"I have been crucified with Christ and I no longer live, but Christ lives in me. The life I now live in the body, I live by faith in the Son of God, who loved me and gave himself for me" (Galatians 2:20).

Sermon series could be preached on this single verse, but here's the nutshell version: The God who breathed the universe into being is alive and well and living in us. Can I hear an amen?

What does this mean for us today?

- He gives patience when the kids push our buttons.
- He gives wisdom for that difficult relationship.
- He gives strength for the task that seems too big.
- He gives hope when every option is exhausted.
- He gives peace when storm winds rage.

Christ, who loves us enough to die for us, promised to never leave us. He fulfilled His promise by sending the Holy Spirit to indwell us. Imagine—the one for whom nothing is impossible lives in us!

Embrace this truth and live today fully alive!

Take Action: Meditate throughout today on this thought: "Christ lives in me."

Dress Rehearsal

Lord, please teach me to worship You continuously.

Our community boasts an amateur live theater. My husband and I enjoy front-row seats because the view provides a close-up of the actors' facial expressions. Their ability to immerse themselves into their onstage characters always amazes me, but I shouldn't be surprised. After all, they've invested countless hours into rehearsals before the program goes public.

Years ago I heard someone say that our lives on earth are dress rehearsals for heaven, where ceaseless worship of Christ, the Lamb, will be the most significant role we play. "Day after day and night after night they keep on saying, 'Holy, holy, holy is the Lord God Almighty—the one who always was, who is, and who is still to come'" (Revelation 4:8 NLT).

We'll want to offer our best performance for the King someday, right? So let's hone our skills now. Let's discipline our minds to carry on continuous conversations with the Lord, praising Him for His power, mercy, and unfailing love.

May our dress rehearsal anticipate the heavenly program yet to come.

Take Action: Fill in the blank with five words or statements: "Father, I praise You for _____."

Free from Idols

Lord, help me keep my heart reserved only for You.

While living in Nepal, we saw people worship cows by adorning them with marigold garlands, placing cooked rice before them, and sprinkling their heads with red powder.

We don't often see idol worship like this in North America, but it exists nonetheless. Anything that usurps God's place in our lives, anything we love more than Him, is an idol.

An idol might be food or fashion. It might be a relationship or hobby. It might be our own bodies, money, careers, or reputations. It might be social media or even ministry.

The latter can become an idol without our realizing it. We must constantly seek to keep God, not the service we do for Him, as our first priority. To ensure nothing edges Him out, we must find our joy in His person and presence more than in the spiritual work we do.

First John 5:21 (NLT) says, "Dear children, keep away from anything that might take God's place in your hearts." God wants and deserves our complete devotion. Let's ensure we give it.

Take Action: Has something taken God's place in your heart? If so, what must you do to reestablish Him as your first love?

Weary

*Lord, help me respond appropriately
when I'm feeling weary.*

How do you behave when you're weary from the inside out? Weariness strikes everyone at one time or another, and when it does—watch out! Even Moses was no exception. Imagine his weariness when the Israelites were at Kadesh. There in the desert, his sister died and was buried. At the same time, the nation faced a crisis—they had no water. The people were so angry, they gathered in opposition against Moses.

Moses prayed, and God gave instructions: "Take the staff and go speak to that rock. The people will see water gush forth for them and their livestock." But Moses only partially obeyed. He took the staff all right, but he used it to hit the rock twice. Disaster.

Water gushed forth, but bone-weary Moses had failed to obey God completely. As a result, God banned him from the Promised Land (Numbers 20:1-13).

God holds us accountable at all times. Weariness doesn't excuse sin. When we are exhausted, let's call on Him for help before doing something inappropriate.

Take Action: Ask the Holy Spirit to control you at all times, especially when you're bone weary.

The Secret to Happiness

Lord, You're my source of happiness.

"Turn to your neighbor, touch your elbow to hers, and let out a hearty laugh," said the keynote speaker at a meeting I recently attended. "Laughter is good medicine, so let's give ourselves a dose."

People desire happiness, but the real deal isn't found in laughter yoga or other man-made counterfeits. Neither is it found in position, possessions, or promises of health and wealth.

Genuine happiness comes when we're in vibrant relationship with God, living in harmony with Him and according to His design.

"For the LORD God is our sun and shield. He gives us grace and glory. The LORD will withhold no good thing from those who do what is right. O LORD of Heaven's Armies, what joy for those who trust in you" (Psalm 84:11-12 NLT).

Knowing God brings contentment, strength, courage, hope, and genuine happiness. There are no shortcuts. There are no alternatives. God created us for intimacy with Himself. Apart from Him, our pursuit of happiness is in vain.

Take Action: Have you sought happiness somewhere other than in knowing God? If so, ask God to restore your heart fully to His.

Significance of One

Lord, make my life count for eternal purposes.

We live in a world filled with capable people doing amazing things. As we listen to reports of their exploits—making medical breakthroughs, defending human trafficking victims, writing bestsellers—it's easy to feel insignificant. This is especially true if we feel our work is mundane or if we've yet to discover our spiritual gifts and passions.

We can also feel insignificant when we look at mankind's endless needs. We think, "I'm just one woman. I can't possibly make a difference in the big scheme of things."

But nothing could be further from the truth. "For we are God's handiwork, created in Christ Jesus to do good works, which God prepared in advance for us to do" (Ephesians 2:10).

God has designed each of us for a specific purpose. It might not have the public presence or far-reaching impact that some have, but it's no less important to Him. Let's never underestimate the influence and significance of one woman completely yielded to God for His highest purpose.

Take Action: Are you doing the good works God prepared for you? If not, what might be holding you back?

Appearances Deceive

Lord, please help me see people as You do.

Outward appearances deceive. I once assumed several tough-looking bikers were Hell's Angels. Actually, they were members of a Christian motorcycle club.

I also mistook a wee white-haired grandma as a withdrawn senior. In reality, she was a spiritual giant fighting jet lag, having just returned from Cambodia, where she oversees a thriving orphanage.

Remember Susan Boyle, the dowdy woman who appeared on *Britain's Got Talent*? Everyone viewed her with skepticism until she sang. Her voice wowed the world.

Sometimes we judge people's character, ability, and worth by their outward appearance. Doing so is unwise and unfair. We need to adopt God's perspective lest we make false assumptions. "The LORD does not look at the things people look at. People look at the outward appearance, but the LORD looks at the heart," says 1 Samuel 16:7.

Let's guard against making false and negative assumptions based on outward appearance. God values people for what's inside, not for what they look like. Let's do the same.

Take Action: Recall an instance when someone's appearance deceived you. What lesson did you learn?

Fishing All Night

Lord, thank You for the encouragement to persevere.

The night had been long for Simon and his fishing buddies on the Sea of Galilee. They'd tossed their nets and hoped for a big haul, but the nets had returned empty. And then Jesus showed up. "Put out into deep water, and let down the nets for a catch," He said.

Simon protested, but only a little. "Master, we've worked hard all night and haven't caught anything. But because you say so, I will let down the nets."

Simon's obedience paid off. "When they had done so, they caught such a large number of fish that their nets began to break...They came and filled both boats so full that they began to sink" (Luke 5:4-7).

Maybe you, too, have been fishing all night. You've cast your nets on behalf of your marriage, hoping your efforts will haul in happiness. You've searched for employment. You've prayed for your prodigal. Your nets are empty, and you're tired. But Jesus says, "Try again."

His words make little sense, but your obedience could make all the difference. Go ahead, toss those nets again.

Take Action: Draw a fishhook and write "Still Fishing, Still Trusting" below it. Put it on your fridge.

Door Crashing

Lord, thank You for direction.

Catherine Marshall writes, "When we ask God to guide us, we have to accept by faith that He is doing so. This means that when He closes a door in our faces, we do well not to try to crash that door." [4]

Marshall is so right! Have you ever tried to crash a God-closed door? I have, but I learned quickly that doing so hurts. Picture a pug-nosed puppy. The aftermath is simply not worth it.

When we ask God for guidance, accepting the outcome He chooses is vital. We dare not ask Him to lead us while inwardly plotting to follow our own desires.

Remembering the character of the One from whom we seek guidance is also vital. He's our Shepherd, who leads us. He closes one gate and opens another because He knows something we don't about what's on the other side.

"He will teach us his ways, so that we may walk in his paths," says Micah 4:2. He guards our best interests, and we need to trust His heart.

Take Action: Ask the Lord to help you respect God-closed doors.

Celebrate

*Lord, You've given me countless
reasons to celebrate You.*

Our society loves to celebrate high achievers. We acknowledge these folks publicly and often reward them with certificates, trophies, promotions, or cash prizes.

My dictionary defines "celebrate" as "to make known publicly; to praise widely." If we celebrate people considered worthy, how much more should we celebrate God?

Someone once said we celebrate God when we think magnificently of Him. This involves three things. First, we acknowledge Him for who He is—the holy and victorious One, the everlasting Father, and the Shepherd of our souls. (This list is highly abbreviated!)

Next, we acknowledge Him for what He does—He creates and sustains life, cleanses us from sin, comforts us, guides us, teaches us, and protects us.

Finally, we offer Him what He deserves—our wholehearted devotion. We can't give Him any physical objects that He doesn't already own, but He wants and deserves our love.

Put these things into practice, and every day will be a true celebration of the best sort.

Take Action: Read Psalm 145 aloud. As you do, celebrate God in your heart.

Inner Strength

Lord, Your mighty power is more than enough.

It was Christmas 1999, and I felt anything but festive. I was beyond exhausted after a topsy-turvy eight weeks prior to the holiday season—our family had moved into a house that desperately needed repair, my dad suffered two crippling strokes, my youngest daughter underwent surgery, and bursitis crippled my left shoulder.

Others around me celebrated Christ's birth while I tried in vain to muster physical and emotional reserve. One day I read Ephesians 3:16—"I pray that from his [God's] glorious, unlimited resources he will empower you with inner strength through his Spirit" (NLT).

This truth became my lifeline. I clung to it, trusting God to fulfill His promise. And He did, one day at a time.

Perhaps you can relate. Your strength, like mine, has dwindled to below zero at times. Be encouraged by knowing that God's resources are infinite. He knows when you're weary, and He'll strengthen you mightily through the power of the Spirit living in you. You just have to ask.

Take Action: Pray Ephesians 3:16, giving thanks in advance—"Father, thank You for Your unlimited resources and for giving me mighty inner strength through Your Holy Spirit. Amen."

I Belong

Lord, thank You for making me belong.

We're born with a desire to belong and be loved. We want to be part of a family, group, or team. Heaven forbid we should be the last one picked for that team.

Anyone longing for acceptance but feeling the sting of rejection will find these words encouraging: "Even before he made the world, God loved us and chose us in Christ to be holy and without fault in his eyes. God decided in advance to adopt us into his own family by bringing us to himself through Jesus Christ. This is what he wanted to do, and it gave him great pleasure" (Ephesians 1:4-5 NLT).

Savor these verses. Words like "loved us," "chose us," "adopt us," and "bringing us to himself" tell how much God cares for us and wants relationship. And then, to erase any doubt, He says His plan to adopt us brings Him great pleasure. Including us in His family is His initiative. We need only say, "Yes, I want to belong."

Have you done so yet?

Take Action: Reread Ephesians 1:4-5. Circle the words that express God's love for you.

Surrounded

Lord, I'm grateful for the power of Your promises.

When bison feel threatened by an enemy, the females surround their young and face outward. The male bison then surround the females. Either sex can weigh up to 2000 pounds, and they all sport deadly horns. What enemy would tangle with such a formidable force?

We face enemies every day—temptation, discouragement, negative self-talk, hurtful memories, and more. Satan loves to use these things against us to make us feel defeated. But the truth says otherwise.

- God surrounds the godly with His favor as with a shield (Psalm 5:12).
- Unfailing love surrounds those who trust the LORD (Psalm 32:10; 33:22 NLT).
- The Lord surrounds His people forever (Psalm 125:2).

Now picture yourself as the enemy approaches. God's shield of favor, His songs of victory, His unfailing love, His tender mercies, and His very presence surround you.

Yes, the enemy stalks, but victory is yours. Let the truth empower you!

Take Action: Write the truths listed above on a card. Post it where you'll see it often.

The Heart of Worship

Lord, please accept all I do today as an act of worship.

Traveling overseas frequently allows me to worship with people from other cultures. In one place, believers kneel silently in massive stone cathedrals decorated with gold filigree and frescoes. In another country, men and women sit on opposite sides of a plain wooden building. The women wear black. No jewelry or makeup is allowed.

Every summer I worship with about 20 Romanian young adults infected with HIV/AIDS. We cram into a meeting room, crank up guitars and drums, and sing for a half hour or more. They clap, beats missing here and there. No one cares. The joy in their eyes matters more than perfect rhythm.

People worship in various ways around the world. But one factor is the same—it isn't about buildings or traditions. It's about coming before God and honoring Him from a pure heart.

"God is spirit, and his worshipers must worship in the Spirit and in truth" (John 4:24). Regardless of our customary form of worship, God focuses on only one thing—our hearts. Let's ensure they're pure before Him.

Take Action: What mundane task must you do today? Offer it as an act of worship.

Mary Matters

Lord, grant me a heart that says yes to You.

God could have chosen any woman on the planet to mother His child. Why, then, did He pick Mary?

This young woman carried dreams in her heart just as we do today. Suddenly God interrupted her life with a mission that required faith to believe the impossible. Imagine—a virgin birth! It guaranteed public shame and rejection and could have led to her death. No one in her right mind would agree.

But Mary did. "I am the Lord's servant. May everything you have said about me come true" (Luke 1:38 NLT). Other women might have flatly refused or asked for time to consider their answer. But Mary immediately agreed despite an unknown future.

God chose Mary to give birth to His Son and raise Him because she lived a surrendered life. She chose to trust Him no matter what, no strings attached.

God values surrendered hearts. If He interrupted your life today, how would you respond?

Take Action: Ask the Holy Spirit to identify any areas in your life that are not yet completely surrendered. Can you give them up? Consider what might be holding you back.

Get Up

Lord, thank You for setting me free from past failures.

Oswald Chambers says sinking into despair is a common human experience when we realize we've missed a magnificent opportunity. He refers to the disciples' experience in the Garden of Gethsemane.[5]

Mere hours before His betrayal and crucifixion, Jesus asked the men to keep watch with Him while He prayed. They fell asleep instead. Three times He checked on them, and three times He found them snoozing. Imagine their feelings of failure after the soldiers arrested their Master.

But Jesus offered hope. He came to the sleeping disciples and said, "Rise! Let us go!" (Matthew 26:46). The opportunity to stand watch with Him was forever lost, but He didn't dwell on that. He turned their focus to the next course of action and told them to get moving.

Perhaps you've missed a magnificent opportunity. You said no when yes was the appropriate response. You waited for the right moment, but the right moment never came. You've regretted it ever since.

Do not linger in despair or disappointment. Ask God what the next course of action is and get moving.

Take Action: Ask God to awaken you to His magnificent opportunities.

What's in Your Hand?

*Lord, please use the tools in my hand
to accomplish Your purposes.*

"How can God use me?"

Perhaps you've asked this question. You want to be an effective kingdom builder but feel you lack training and skills. Others seem more talented or equipped. Ask yourself this question instead: "What's in my hand?"

Moses doubted his ability to lead the Israelites from captivity. "What's in your hand?" God asked him.

"A staff," Moses replied.

"Use it," said God (Exodus 4:2).

David, the shepherd boy, held a slingshot and five smooth stones. With these he tumbled Goliath.

What's in your hand?

Perhaps you hold color crayons and finger paints. You have a big heart for little kids and provide a nurturing environment for them to learn and grow.

Maybe you hold scissors. You're a hair stylist, and you offer a listening ear and encouraging words to your clients.

Perhaps you hold a recipe book. You share meals with families in crisis, or you practice hospitality in your home.

What's in your hand? Use it to build God's kingdom.

Take Action: What's one activity you enjoy doing? How can you use that to bless others?

Divine Design

*Lord, please grant me appreciation
for Your divine design.*

Many of us struggle to accept ourselves. Either we don't like the way we look or we're unhappy with our abilities. Comparing ourselves with others only makes matters worse. Before long, we feel substandard and begin doubting our worth.

Scripture says that knowing the truth sets us free (John 8:32). In this case, knowing the truth sets us free to be who God made us to be. So, what is that truth? God divinely designed each one of us. "You created my inmost being; you knit me together in my mother's womb" (Psalm 139:13).

We might feel tempted to say, "Why, then, did You knit me with frizzy hair and no musical abilities?" But let's not do this. It only leads to further discontent.

Instead, let's respond as the psalmist did. "I praise you because I am fearfully and wonderfully made; your works are wonderful, I know that full well" (verse 14). Let's trust that God made no mistakes when He designed us, and let's tell Him so.

God created Adam and said, "It is very good." He says the same about you.

Take Action: Look at your reflection and thank God for creating you.

Clean

Lord, thanks for seeing me through eyes of love.

Two young women approached me at a conference where I was to speak. "Do you know who we are?" they asked.

Their question implied that I should know them, so I studied their faces for a few moments. Sure enough— they'd been my students at a private school more than 20 years prior.

"Of course," I said.

"We were afraid of that," they replied. "Then you probably remember all the trouble we got into."

I did. But that day I saw these gals in a new light. Once rebellious teens, they'd grown into beautiful and confident women.

Many women have a past they'd rather forget. Thankfully, God forgives when we confess. And when He does, He sees us in a new light. In His eyes, we're no longer covered in sin's filth but clothed in His righteousness.

"Do not remember the rebellious sins of my youth. Remember me in the light of your unfailing love, for you are merciful, O LORD," says Psalm 25:7 (NLT). What a joy to know God sees us as clean rather than condemned.

Take Action: Ask God to help you see others as He does.

Choose Life

Lord, please help me make choices that breed life.

Every day presents us with umpteen choices. Some are amoral—neither right nor wrong. The foods we eat, the route we take to work, or the time we go to bed fall into that category.

But some choices are moral. These deserve utmost attention because they can determine the direction of our lives. Here are some examples.

- Should I flirt with that guy who treats me better than my husband does?
- Should I lie on my résumé?
- Should I forgive that person who wounded me?

God created us with the freedom to make choices. Knowing our tendency to make bad ones, He tells us that He's set before us life and death, blessings and curses. Then He gives this caution: "Choose life, so that you and your children may live" (Deuteronomy 30:19).

What choices do you face today? Do not make hasty decisions based on emotion. Rather, pray and consider your options in light of God's word. Then act accordingly and with confidence.

Take Action: Ask a godly friend for prayer if you're struggling with a difficult choice.

Our Mission

Lord, please shine Your light through me.

Hastings Street—possibly the worst neighborhood in Vancouver, British Columbia. Men and women of all ages mired in drug addiction, alcoholism, and prostitution stagger, loiter, and fight. Darkness and despair hover like impenetrable fog. And yet into this darkness shines the light of Christ's followers as they ladle hot soup and provide safe shelter for those in need.

"I will make you a light to the Gentiles, and you will bring my salvation to the ends of the earth," says Isaiah 49:6. That's our mandate as believers—to be a spiritual beacon to those lost in sin's darkness.

The lost aren't found only on Hastings Street. They live on our streets too. They work with us. Attend school with us. They even attend our churches. They come in all shapes, sizes, and colors. They speak every language.

People who don't know Jesus as Savior live in spiritual darkness and need the light. Let's resolve to be that light by loving the lost and entering their worlds rather than waiting for them to enter ours.

Take Action: Consider how you can be intentional about developing a friendship with an unbeliever if you don't already have one.

God's Everywhere Presence

Lord, thanks for surrounding me with Your presence.

My husband and I fly overseas several times each year for ministry purposes. As we wing across the ocean, I meditate on Psalm 139.

"You go before me and follow me...I can never escape from your Spirit! I can never get away from your presence!...If I ride the wings of the morning, if I dwell by the farthest oceans, even there your hand will guide me, and your strength will support me" (Psalm 139:5-10 NLT).

Personalizing these verses embeds the truth of God's presence in my head and heart. "If I spend the summer ministering at evangelistic camps in Poland and working among HIV-infected youth in Romania, even there Your hand will guide me, and Your strength will support me."

Now it's your turn. Where are you today? Perhaps you're home with sick kids or in a corporate office, hospital, or school. Wherever you go, God precedes and follows you. His hand will guide you, and His strength will support you.

Go in confidence, my friend. God is with you.

Take Action: Personalize Psalm 139:5-10 to fit your situation as I did mine.

Thirsty

Lord, thank You for quenching my spiritual thirst.

Romania can be hot in July. Temperatures often hover between 90 and 115 degrees. Fresh from British Columbia, my body isn't accustomed to this heat. It glistens (female version of "sweats") and begs for water to rehydrate. Satisfying my thirst becomes an all-day endeavor.

David compared physical thirst with spiritual thirst while in the desert of Judah. He wrote, "You, God, are my God, earnestly I seek you; I thirst for you, my whole being longs for you, in a dry and parched land where there is no water" (Psalm 63:1).

Our bodies need water to survive. Without it, our cells dehydrate and die. Likewise, our souls need Christ—the living water—to survive. He alone satisfies our spiritual thirst (John 4:13-14). Without Him, we die.

In the midst of our busy lives, we commonly try to quench our spiritual thirst with teeny sips on the run. But our souls need more. Let's make time to sit, drink deeply from Christ, and experience His life-giving refreshment.

He alone satisfies our thirst.

Take Action: Drink a glass of water and acknowledge Christ as the living water.

Integrity

Lord, please help me be faithful in all things.

What's integrity worth nowadays? Not so much, according to whoever leaves messages on my phone saying I've won yet another cruise. Or Ponzi schemers who bilk seniors out of their savings. Or athletes who win medals through illegal doping.

But Scripture says otherwise. "A good name is more desirable than great riches; to be esteemed is better than silver or gold" (Proverbs 22:1).

Your reputation as a woman of integrity is priceless. Once lost, it's difficult to regain. Therefore, we must guard it well, beginning with things such things as returning extra change when a clerk miscounts, not watching inappropriate online or television content, and avoiding compromising situations with members of the opposite sex.

As women of integrity, we choose the high road even though the low road is easier and brings instant gratification. Integrity keeps us pure and honest. It's what we are when no one is watching.

What's your integrity worth? And what are you doing to protect it?

Take Action: Have you compromised your integrity in any way? If so, make it right with God and man. Ask God for the courage to maintain integrity from now on.

Every Moment Matters

Lord, teach me to approach each day fully alive.

Gene and I were driving when I began feeling chest pain. Within minutes I felt nauseous and light-headed. We knew these symptoms were serious, so we drove to the nearest hospital.

An emergency room nurse popped a nitroglycerin tablet under my tongue. Then she ran several tests and phoned for an EKG. "Hurry," she said. "This one shows cardiac signs."

The EKG showed nothing wrong. A chest x-ray and blood tests confirmed those results. A treadmill test several days later showed that my heart was fine.

My family doctor looked at the reports and said, "I don't know what happened. It's a mystery."

I don't know what happened either, but one thing's for sure. This situation showed me how life can change in a heartbeat. We need to cherish every moment and not waste any on trivial pursuits.

"Teach us to realize the brevity of life, so that we may grow in wisdom," says Psalm 90:12 (NLT). Indeed, let's make each moment count. Let's live life to the full, investing in what matters for eternity.

Take Action: What would you change about your life if you knew it would soon end?

God Notices

*Lord, thanks for seeing and noting
hidden acts of kindness.*

A newspaper contains a column titled "Roses." It acknowledges locals who perform acts of kindness, such as returning a lost wallet with contents intact or changing a senior's flat tire.

Publicly thanking those who do random acts of kindness is a great idea. It provides a warm fuzzy feeling of being appreciated, and who doesn't like that?

But what if you extend kindness anonymously? Or for someone who spurns your efforts? What if you do selfless acts behind the scenes day in and day out with nary a nod or thank-you? Parents and caregivers of young children know the feeling. So do those caring for seniors and folks with special needs. Countless others can relate.

Here's an encouragement for those whose kindness doesn't make the "Roses" column. "God is not unjust; he will not forget your work and the love you have shown him as you have helped his people and continue to help them" (Hebrews 6:10). You might feel as though your work is overlooked, but it's not. God sees your labor of love, and He will reward you.

Take Action: Send an encouraging card to someone whose work is often overlooked.

Offer Your Lunch

Lord, here's my little offering.

Writing for publication was an act of obedience for me. I returned from my first writers' conference feeling completely inadequate, but the conviction that God was calling me compelled me to move forward.

I prayed about this endeavor every day for months. I always ended with the prayer, "God, I feel inadequate for this task, but You're more than enough. I offer You my meager skills and knowledge. Take them, multiply them as You did the disciples' little lunch, and feed the masses."

I based my prayer on Matthew 15:32-38. Jesus and His disciples were in a remote place ministering to thousands. Three days passed, and Jesus wanted to feed them. The disciples asked, "Where could we get enough bread?"

Jesus answered, "How many loaves do you have?"

The answer: "Seven...and a few small fish." That was enough for Jesus. He took the meager, worked a miracle, and fed the masses.

What is God asking you to do? Don't worry about what you don't have. Offer Him what you do have and watch Him do something amazing.

Take Action: With palms facing up, offer your time and talents to God.

My Light

Lord, thank You for bringing light into my life.

Our family lived on an island off the coast of British Columbia for 11 years. Winter windstorms were commonplace, and they invariably knocked out the electricity. On one occasion, wind damage plunged us into darkness for five days.

There I was, cooking dinner on a barbecue grill in the carport after dark, holding a flashlight in one hand while checking chicken breasts for doneness with the other.

Relief understates how I felt when the power was restored and the lights returned. My spirits brightened. My attitude improved. And life in general seemed easier. The same is true in the spiritual realm when Jesus, the light of the world, enters our lives.

The psalmist expresses it well: "You light a lamp for me. The LORD, my God, lights up my darkness. In your strength I can crush an army; with my God I can scale any wall" (Psalm 18:28-29 NLT).

Christ in us dispels the darkness of sin and despair. He brings hope, peace, and joy. He lifts our burdens and makes life seem easier. How blessed we are to know Jesus—the light of the world.

Take Action: Pray Psalm 18:28-29 with gratitude.

Persistence in Prayer

Lord, please help me never give up in prayer.

Praying persistently means presenting our requests to God over and over and over again, sometimes for years without seeing a response. How many of us are willing to persevere to that degree?

Waiting for extended times for God to answer prayer requires patience. It also requires trust in His sovereignty and timing. He may be orchestrating divine details behind the scenes. Our request will appear to go unanswered until those details align to accomplish His purposes.

Jesus told a parable about a woman who repeatedly asked the local judge to administer justice against her adversary. Her persistence paid off, and the judge finally listened to her pleas (Luke 18:1-8). Jesus told this story to show the disciples "that they should always pray and not give up."

The same principle applies to us today. Let's pray and not give up hope for that prodigal child to return. For that broken marriage to be restored. For a financial breakthrough. And for a loved one's salvation.

What is your request to God? Pray and never give up.

Take Action: Commit to praying persistently for the salvation of an unbelieving friend.

Secret to a Great Day

Lord, thanks for the gift of today.

How do you greet the morning? Maybe you smack the snooze button on the alarm, groan, and roll over to catch a few more winks. Or perhaps you wake with a song in your heart and a spring in your step. Regardless, today is a God-sent gift, so live it fully alive.

How so? Colossians 2:6-7 explains. "Just as you received Christ Jesus as Lord, continue to live your lives in him, rooted and built up in him, strengthened in the faith as you were taught, and overflowing with thankfulness."

Here's what this looks like in practical terms.

- Spend time alone with the Lord. Doing so aligns your heart with His and helps you understand His purpose for you today.
- Practice God's presence. Invite Him into every moment, even the mundane.
- Utilize God's strength for whatever comes. You needn't try to cope in your own power.
- Practice thanksgiving in every circumstance.

Regardless of what today brings, make it your goal to live in Christ Jesus. If you do this, your day will be great.

Take Action: Commit Colossians 2:6-7 to memory.

God's Word—My Delight

Lord, thanks for the treasure of Your written word.

The Scriptures are our key to fruitful, blessed lives. They warn, encourage, and instruct us. Studying and understanding them is vital to understanding God's mind and values and to living lives that He honors. Sadly, sometimes we neglect them and focus on other pursuits.

Personally, I struggle with time issues. (I'll bet you can relate.) I've learned that my Bible reading must happen early in the morning before I write, check emails, do household chores, or run errands. Postponing it guarantees it won't happen. All too quickly, a day without God's word rolls into another and another as other activities usurp the rightful place of Scripture. My Bible sits abandoned while I reason, "I'll make time for you tomorrow."

Psalm 119:14,16 says, "I rejoice in following your statues as one rejoices in great riches...I delight in your decrees; I will not neglect your word."

Let the psalmist's words be true about our love for God's word. May we rejoice in it as in great riches. May we delight in reading it. And may we never neglect it.

Take Action: Listen to a CD of Scripture set to music.

Heavenly Citizenship

*Lord, thank You for the privilege of citizenship
in Your heavenly kingdom.*

I am a Canadian citizen, and I consider that a privilege. So do people from other countries I visit. "From Canada?" they say. "You're very lucky. Yours is a good country. A rich country." And then comes a second question: "How can I immigrate to Canada?"

If only I could help them.

In the physical realm, our citizenship lies in the country our passport denotes. But Christ's followers have a second citizenship—in heaven, where God dwells and where death, sickness, and pain do not exist (Philippians 3:20; Revelation 21:3-4).

Gaining earthly citizenship is often a lengthy process. But gaining citizenship in heaven requires only one thing: placing our trust in Jesus Christ alone for salvation.

We have daily contact with people who aren't yet citizens of heaven. Are they aware of the opportunity? Do they understand how simple it is?

Let's ask the Lord to bring people into our lives who are not yet citizens of heaven but who are ready to pursue this amazing opportunity.

Take Action: Pray daily for the salvation of an unbelieving relative or friend.

Listen

*Lord, please grant me a heart
that listens well to Your voice.*

Listening is a skill that many could improve. Recently I was working on a manuscript at the kitchen table when my daughter came home from school. She talked about her new semester schedule and classes.

I thought I listened, but when she left the room, I realized I hadn't heard a word she said. My mind was on my manuscript, not on my daughter's words.

Listening well means we set aside preoccupations so we can focus on what another person says. It also means we listen respectfully, not interrupting or punctuating the conversation with eye rolls.

The psalmist wrote, "I will listen to what God the Lord says" (Psalm 85:8). God wants to speak to us, and we need to open our ears and our hearts to truly hear His words.

Doing so might require setting aside work to focus on reading His word or pausing in prayer to capture His whispers. It takes effort, just as learning to listen well in conversation with others does, but communication with God is worth it. Agreed?

Take Action: Withdraw to a solitary place for five minutes today and listen for God's voice.

Suffering

*Lord, please teach me to regard suffering
as a means to refine my faith.*

The common response to suffering is resistance. That's understandable because pain of all types is unpleasant. Who welcomes something that hurts? When suffering comes our way, we often pray for God to remove it. Perhaps we ought to think again.

The apostle Peter encouraged believers to adopt a different perspective about suffering and trials. "These have come so that the proven genuineness of your faith—of greater worth than gold, which perishes even though refined by fire—may result in praise, glory and honor when Jesus Christ is revealed" (1 Peter 1:7).

The prodigal son experienced famine and financial loss. His suffering changed his selfishness to humility and resulted in reunion with his father. Our circumstances, though different from his, can either drive us from our heavenly Father or send us running to His embrace. It's our choice.

Are you or a loved one suffering today? Rather than praying for the pain to be removed, ask God to use it to refine you and bring glory to Himself.

Take Action: Apply 1 Thessalonians 5:18 to your situation today by giving thanks in all circumstances.

A Continual Feast

Lord, thank You for providing a feast for my soul.

Imagine a huge banquet loaded with delectables to please every palate. All calorie-free.

Now imagine a fast-food meal.

Which meal would you rather eat?

"For the happy heart, life is a continual feast," says Proverbs 15:15 (NLT). Unfortunately we sometimes settle for the burger and fries. We allow life's disappointments and daily grind to bog us down, and our hearts feel anything but happy. But we can change that!

We can enjoy a continual feast of the soul by living each day with an awareness of and gratitude for…

- God's presence. Knowing we're never alone brings comfort.
- God's power. Knowing nothing is impossible for Him brings courage.
- God's promises. Knowing He'll do what He says brings confidence.

Focusing on these truths guarantees a happy heart—one that's rooted in peace and contentment.

Take Action: Find a Scripture promise that's relevant to you today and memorize it.

Confidence

*Lord, thank You for the confidence
that comes from knowing You.*

Our local amateur theater recently featured a production titled *Mary's Wedding*. One actor portrayed a World War I soldier who, though terrified of thunderstorms and of fighting in the trenches, mustered enough courage to charge through enemy lines on horseback.

Fear is common to all mankind, and we choose how to respond to it. We can either let it paralyze us or face it head-on and grow as a result.

The psalmist experienced fear, but he refused to let it control him. Instead, he found courage in God. "The LORD is my light and my salvation—so why should I be afraid?" he wrote. "Though a mighty army surrounds me, my heart will not be afraid. Even if I am attacked, I will remain confident" (Psalm 27:1,3 NLT).

Sometimes we feel as though we're in the trenches and under attack. That's when we need to recall the psalmist's words. Though a mighty army surrounds us, we need not fear. Confidence is ours because the Lord is our salvation.

Take Action: When you feel afraid, talk to God, saying, "You are my light and salvation—so why should I be afraid?"

God Is Good

Lord, I praise You for being good—all the time.

A familiar table grace says, "God is great. God is good. Let us thank Him for this food. Amen." We can recite this ditty mindlessly when our needs are supplied and our circumstances easy. It takes more thought when the table is empty or life serves a raw deal.

Applying head knowledge to real life is tough when emotions ask, is God really great? Is He really good? If He is, why doesn't He just zap our hurts to make them disappear?

We don't know why God doesn't make our hurts vanish, and He owes us no explanation. But He does ask us to trust Him because of who He is. "You are good, and what you do is good" (Psalm 119:68).

"God is great. God is good." These words are not to be recited flippantly. They carry life-changing truths. God *is* great. And by nature He *is* good. Therefore what He does is also good. Do you believe this?

Take Action: Recite the prayer above but tweak the last sentence. "God is great. God is good. I will thank Him for _____."

Verbal Legacy

Lord, please fill my mouth with songs about You.

What type of verbal legacy do you want to leave for your kids, grandkids, nieces, and nephews—even the children in your church family?

I've visited homes where mothers' words consisted mainly of criticism and complaining. Call it toxic talk if you wish. How much healthier their families would be if these moms realized their mouths' potential for good.

Now that I'm a grandmother and realize afresh the impressionability of children's minds, I'm determined to speak words that honor the Lord and whet others' appetites for Him. Psalm 89:1-2 describes my desire— "I will sing of the LORD's great love forever; with my mouth I will make your faithfulness known through all generations. I will declare that your love stands firm forever, that you have established your faithfulness in heaven itself."

I don't want to start sermonizing. Rather, I want to seize teachable moments to share biblical truth, tell personal stories about God's faithfulness in my life, and encourage my family to love the Lord wholeheartedly.

Let's choose to use our mouths to show love for God with the prayer that others will love Him too.

Take Action: Sing a favorite worship chorus.

Avoid Error

Lord, please protect me from falling into spiritual error.

The Sadducees were a religious sect comprised mainly of priests and aristocrats. They discounted oral traditions and said there was no resurrection of the dead. One day they confronted Jesus with a trick question about the afterlife. This revealed their lack of understanding the truth.

Jesus replied, "You are in error because you do not know the Scriptures or the power of God" (Matthew 22:29).

Unfortunately, believers today sometimes fall into error too. Neglecting the study of God's word can result in our misinterpreting the Scriptures. It can also result in worldly philosophies or wrong teaching, leading us astray. Before long we buy into the gospel according to popular talk-show hosts or self-help programs.

Knowing the truth according to God's written word is vital for us as believers. So is maintaining our personal relationship with Jesus Christ. The more vibrant that relationship, the more sure-footed we are in our faith, and the less likely we are to fall into error.

Take Action: Ask God to show you if you've adopted any worldly philosophies as gospel truth. If you have, compare them with God's truth and turn from them.

God Is on Our Side

Lord, thanks for being my cheerleader.

For years Karyn dreamed of developing scent-free skin care products. She researched, crunched numbers, and prayed for direction. Finally she sensed God say, "Now." One afternoon, Karyn told her sister of her plans to move forward.

Her sister gave a halfhearted smile. "Good luck," she said. "You're going to have a steep learning curve. Hopefully, your dream won't tank."

"You're right—there is a lot to learn," said Karyn. "I'm a bit nervous, but I can either fixate on the unknowns or I can focus on the truth. God is on my side. What more do I need?"

Romans 8:31 (NLT) says, "If God is for us, who can ever be against us?" Family and friends might ridicule, criticize, or reject us. Circumstances might not appear favorable toward us. But none of that matters in light of this fact: God is for us!

Imagine—the Creator of the universe cheers for you. He's got your back. He's on your side, sister. You can do anything He asks you to do when you're walking in right relationship with Him.

Take Action: What's your greatest challenge today? Thank God for being on your side and then face it with confidence.

Blessings

Lord, I'm grateful for Your kindness to me.

In the midst of our busy lives, we do ourselves a favor by pausing to reflect on our blessings. This exercise opens our eyes to gifts we might otherwise take for granted. And it humbles us by revealing how very privileged we are.

"Who am I, O Sovereign Lord, and what is my family, that you have brought me this far?" asked King David (2 Samuel 7:18). When we begin to name our blessings, we ask the same question. "Who are we that You should bring us this far?"

Who are we to sleep in warmth and security when others are homeless? Who are we to eat three meals a day and still have leftovers when others scrounge for food? Who are we to receive medical care when others ride piggyback on loved ones for several days to the nearest doctor? Who are we to live in a democracy when others are oppressed by tyrants?

Surely we are blessed far beyond what we deserve. Let's determine to cultivate gratitude not only for the obvious but also for the gifts we might otherwise overlook.

Take Action: List at least five blessings you haven't acknowledged until now.

In His Thoughts

Lord, I'm humbled when I consider that You're constantly mindful of me.

My husband and I met while serving at a Christian summer camp. The summer ended all too soon but not before we'd fallen in love and decided to marry the following February. Trouble was, Gene lived in Washington state, and I lived in Alberta. Nearly 800 miles separated us.

We saw each other only four times during our engagement, but we thought about each other continuously. Cards and letters proved it. So did our phone bills.

When we love others deeply, we think about them often. Imagine, then, what Psalm 139:17-18 declares about God's passion for us. "How precious to me are your thoughts, God! How vast is the sum of them! Were I to count them, they would outnumber the grains of sand—when I awake, I am still with you."

You might wonder sometimes whether God is thinking about you, but let these words dispel all doubts. Truth is, you're on His mind front and center this very moment because He's wild about you. Do you believe it?

Take Action: Write the words "God is thinking about me" on several Post-it notes and post them around your house.

Wait

Lord, teach me to wait well.

Sometimes "wait" feels like a four-letter word. We see something (or someone) we want—a job, a new house, upgraded education, motherhood, a ministry opportunity, better health—and take steps to attain it. But God stops the process. "Wait," He says.

Wait? But I want it now. Why can't I have it now?

There's a reason for waiting, says Lamentations 3:25 (NASB). "The LORD is good to those who wait for Him, to the person who seeks Him."

God knows every detail of our lives. He knows when we're ready for change, and He knows when the change is ready for us. He works behind the scenes in us and around us on a timeline we don't understand. And so we must trust Him.

Let's make the wait a positive experience. Let's remain faithful where we are, seeking to know God more intimately and striving to learn the lessons He has for us during that time.

"Wait" is indeed a four-letter word, and that word is good.

Take Action: Memorize Lamentations 3:26—"It is good to wait quietly for the salvation of the Lord."

Peace

Lord, thank You for being my peace.

Today's worries and tomorrow's fears can hold us hostage because we tend to entertain what-ifs and worst-case scenarios. Stress increases. Sleep decreases. And anxiety makes us sick.

Sigh. If only we could find peace.

Good news—we can! But we won't find it by trying to control our circumstances. Neither will we find it by denying those circumstances or by trying to escape or drown them. Peace comes from a person—Jesus Christ. "For he himself is our peace," says Ephesians 2:14.

Knowing Christ intimately causes us to trust Him implicitly. Friendship with Him begins when we acknowledge Him as Savior. Intimacy develops as with in-the-flesh relationships—by spending time together. It grows as we learn more about Him through God's word. And it deepens when we walk in obedience to His commands.

The more we know Christ—the more we allow Him to fill and control us with the Holy Spirit—the more peace we experience.

Peace is a person. Focus on Him, and peace is yours.

Take Action: Using PEACE as an acronym, name five characteristics of Christ that are especially meaningful to you.

True Wealth

Lord, make me wealthy in Your eyes.

Society equates wealth with material abundance. But a storehouse of money and stuff has nothing to do with true wealth. Rather, it's found in having peace of heart and tranquility of mind. In a word, it's found in contentment.

Contentment comes when we realize God's sovereignty in our lives. We recognize that He's created us in a particular way. He's planted us in a specific place. He's surrounded us with particular people. And we're at rest.

There's no angst. No envy. No striving for more. And no desire to escape or change our circumstances. That's contentment—a treasure, a virtue no amount of money can buy.

"Better a little with righteousness than much gain with injustice," says Proverbs 16:8. Being at peace with our Maker—that's wealth. So is making memories with family and friends, living fully alive with no regrets, and living a life that whets others' appetites for Jesus.

Never let society convince you that wealth and material abundance are synonymous. Develop a contented heart, and you'll experience wealth in the truest sense of the word.

Take Action: Are you wrestling with God's doings in your life? Ask Him for contentment.

Endure Well

Lord, teach me to persevere with a smile.

Everyone deals with disappointments and trials. But not everyone deals with them in the same way.

Some try to cope using relaxation techniques, medication, or alcohol.

Some get mad. They vent their anger at God. "You're not fair!" they say. "How can a loving God allow this to happen?"

But some turn to the same God others spurn. They cry to Him, admit their helplessness, seek comfort, and ask for strength. They honor God as they persevere through the tough stuff, and God honors them for their response. "God blesses those who patiently endure testing and temptation. Afterward they will receive the crown of life that God has promised to those who love him" (James 1:12 NLT).

Anyone can respond to trials negatively. But only the spiritually mature can endure with patience and an attitude of surrender and humility.

Personally, I don't enjoy tests. But I know that God blesses and rewards those who respond with patience, and that motivates me to endure well. How about you?

Take Action: Evaluate your response to testing. How does it measure up to God's standard of patient endurance?

Prayer and a Pure Heart

*Lord, thanks for showing me how to have
an unhindered prayer life.*

I argued with God for a year when I sensed Him telling me to write *Moving from Fear to Freedom: A Woman's Guide to Peace in Every Situation.* Every time I read my Bible and prayed, the heavens felt like brass.

My disobedience was the cause, and I knew it. Everything changed the moment I confessed my disobedience as sin and said yes to writing the book.

God is holy and cannot tolerate sin in our lives. We fool ourselves if we think we can disobey Him without consequences. One of those consequences is that He will not hear our prayers. "If I had cherished sin in my heart, the Lord would not have listened" (Psalm 66:18).

The good news is, God promises to forgive us when we confess our sin (1 John 1:9). And when our hearts are pure before Him, we know He hears our prayers and will answer.

Sin hinders prayer. Let's commit to maintaining pure hearts so this will not be true of us.

Take Action: Ask God to reveal sin in your life. When He does, make the appropriate course correction.

Watching Our Words

*Lord, please teach me
to speak only wholesome words.*

Women usually speak about 20,000 words daily. We talk about our new shoes, recipes, and Pinterest. We compliment a friend's hairdo. Remind our kids to do their homework. Tell our spouses we love them.

That's all good. Trouble is, sometimes we spend a few thousand words on criticism, gossip, and venting. "Thanks for listening," we say. "It feels good to get that off my chest."

Sometimes we speak negative words. Sometimes we listen to others speak negative words. Regardless, we ought to make Ephesians 4:29 our goal: "Do not let any unwholesome talk come out of your mouths, but only what is helpful for building others up according to their needs, that it may benefit those who listen."

Let's take this instruction to heart. Before we open our mouths to speak, let's ask, are my words wholesome? Are they helpful? Do they build others up?

Let's choose our words well and use them to bless and benefit others.

Take Action: Ask God to make you ultrasensitive to the words you speak before you open your mouth.

Easily Identified

Lord, please make it obvious that I'm Yours.

Everyone who joins us on a short-term ministry trip receives a shirt that features the logo of International Messengers. We ask people to wear the shirts while en route to their overseas destination. Why?

The reason is simple—participants often fly from various airports into London, where they meet and catch a flight together to their final stop. Sometimes team members have not yet met in person, so the shirts make them easily recognizable as members of the same organization.

In the spiritual realm, believers wear evidence of belonging to the same team too. In this case, love is the logo. Jesus said, "By this everyone will know that you are my disciples, if you love one another" (John 13:35).

Anyone can love others who are easy to love, but only those empowered by the Holy Spirit can truly love as Christ did—selflessly and sacrificially—when the going gets tough. The ability to do so sets us apart. Others can easily identify us as His followers.

We're members of Christ's family. Let's wear the love logo well.

Take Action: Ask God to show you how to demonstrate love to someone who can never repay you—and then do it.

Love Your Enemies

Lord, please help me behave as Your child.

Anyone can love a kind neighbor, coworker, or family member. But most of us find it challenging to love and pray for those who mistreat us. We'd rather steer clear or give them what they deserve. We might even feel a bit smug if they fall on hard times.

People haven't changed much since Jesus' day. He recognized the same attitudes and behaviors, and He confronted and challenged them. "You have heard the law that says, 'Love your neighbor' and hate your enemy. But I say, love your enemies! Pray for those who persecute you! In that way, you will be acting as true children of your Father in heaven" (Matthew 5:43-45 NLT).

As children of God, we're to rise to a higher standard—one that's unattainable in our own strength. Any woman can love a friend, but it takes a woman under the Holy Spirit's control to truly care about an enemy. It seems impossible, but if God commands it, then He enables it.

Take Action: How do you treat your enemies? Ask God to reveal His love to them through you.

Bloom

*Lord, please grant me a grateful heart
in the here and now.*

A familiar quote says, "Bloom where you're planted."
God spoke this phrase to me when I was 24 years
old and planted in a Nepalese village of 70 people. Electricity, indoor plumbing, telephones, and laptops were
nonexistent there. I felt isolated, homesick, and heartsick.

One morning I heard a quiet voice whisper, "Bloom
where you're planted." And so I did—by learning to
give thanks.

"Thank You, God," I prayed daily, "for our neighbors' hospitality, for the beauty of our surroundings,
for the quiet of this village, and for giving me this rich
cross-cultural experience." I thanked God for rain and
sunshine, for the way He met our basic needs, and for
anything else that came to mind. Within a few months,
I truly enjoyed living there.

Let's not wait for circumstances to change before
putting our heart into whatever we're doing in that
place. Instead, let's do as Psalm 105:1 says—"Give
praise to the LORD, proclaim his name"—and our souls
will prosper.

Take Action: Think of one thing for which to be thankful in your current situation.

No Condemnation

Lord, thank You for freedom.

Little voices haunt us. They remind us of our past failures—sins committed, thoughts entertained, and promises broken. They whisper condemnation…

- "If only you'd done such and such."
- "You should have known better."
- "You can't do anything right. You're worthless."

Condemnation finds its source in Satan, the enemy who seeks to steal, kill, and destroy. He uses it as a weapon against us. A force to drive us to despair. A wedge to separate us from God.

But Scripture tells us the truth. "Now there is no condemnation for those who belong to Christ Jesus. And because you belong to him, the power of the life-giving Spirit has freed you from the power of sin that leads to death" (Romans 8:1-2 NLT).

Satan condemns, but let's not succumb to his efforts. We've been set free from condemnation through Jesus Christ's death and resurrection. He removed our shackles of shame and guilt, and we need never wear them again.

We're forgiven and free. Let the truth negate those little voices.

Take Action: Memorize Romans 8:1-2 to counteract thoughts of condemnation.

Criticism

Lord, teach me to handle criticism graciously.

onest criticism is hard to take, particularly from a relative, a friend, an acquaintance, or a stranger," wrote Franklin P. Jones.

No one enjoys receiving criticism. It's easy to feel picked on or become defensive. However, we benefit by listening and then responding positively when it's warranted.

Offering constructive criticism can be difficult too. We risk the possibility of jeopardizing relationships, but sometimes others need our viewpoint in order to succeed.

Knowing how to handle criticism—both giving and receiving—is important because we'll encounter both sides sooner or later. Let's ask God to grant us humility, put a guard over our tongues, and love others through us.

Proverbs 27:5-6 (NLT) says, "An open rebuke is better than hidden love! Wounds from a sincere friend are better than many kisses from an enemy." Criticism is often considered a negative thing, but it needn't be so. If it helps us or others overcome weak spots and succeed, then it's positive. Let's learn to deal with it appropriately.

Take Action: How do you naturally respond when criticized? What can you learn from this response?

A Dynamic Wardrobe

*Lord, please help me to be a woman who is
clothed in strength and dignity.*

I recently met a professional wardrobe consultant. She
evaluates women's clothes and accessories and then
recommends specific colors and styles best suited for
their needs and body type.

"What you wear matters," she said. "People notice
and they develop an opinion about you."

Our choice of apparel is important, but even more
important is the character with which we clothe ourselves. What do people notice about us? What opinion
do they develop about us, based on what they see of our
actions and attitudes?

Proverbs 31:25 tells of a woman who clothes herself
in strength and dignity. When others look at her, they
see someone who exudes quiet confidence. They notice
her attitude of contentment and her gracious spirit that
puts others first. They see her compassion for others'
needs, the wisdom in her words, the joy in her outlook.

These character qualities are the natural overflow
of the Holy Spirit's control, and they reflect Christ to a
watching word. Talk about a dynamic wardrobe!

Take Action: Name one character quality you wish to
clothe yourself in today. Ask the Holy Spirit to accomplish this.

Search Me

Lord, search my heart and make me clean.

Spending several months in a wheelchair meant seeing life from a new angle. Literally. From this vantage point, I discovered that my house wasn't as clean as I thought it was. I was shocked to see dust bunnies, fingerprints, and smudges I'd not noticed prior to my accident.

Likewise, in the spiritual realm, God uses people and situations in our lives to reveal attitudes and behaviors to which we're oblivious. Pride, envy, jealousy, impure thoughts, impatience...these and more stain our hearts. They need to be removed for us to enjoy unhindered fellowship with God and gain full access to His power for our lives. And so spiritual housekeeping beckons.

Let's invite God to reveal sins to which we've grown accustomed or of which we're unaware. "Search me, O God, and know my heart...See if there is any offensive way in me, and lead me in the way everlasting" (Psalm 139:23-24).

We might be shocked at what He reveals, but let's respond immediately by asking Him to cleanse us and make us pure vessels.

Take Action: Pray Psalm 139:23-24. Listen for the Holy Spirit's response. What is He saying?

A Clean Heart

Lord, please make me aware of sin in my life.

Annette didn't see what others saw in her. A natural leader, she loved overseeing committees at church and her kids' school. Trouble was, her overbearing manner often hurt others.

A friend drew Annette aside after a particularly difficult meeting and tactfully suggested showing more respect. An intense conversation followed during which Annette recognized pride as an issue in her life. She confessed it as sin and began allowing the Holy Spirit to change her.

Sometimes we're blind to our sin. Other times we know it's there but choose to turn a blind eye. Nevertheless, the fact remains—sin is sin, and we can't hide it from God.

The psalmist wrote, "How can I know all the sins lurking in my heart? Cleanse me from these hidden faults. Keep your servant from deliberate sins! Don't let them control me. Then I will be free of guilt and innocent of great sin" (Psalm 19:12-13 NLT).

Let's adopt the psalmist's prayer. Doing so ensures we'll enjoy the blessings of living with pure hearts.

Take Action: Invite the Holy Spirit to identify any sins lurking in your heart today.

Fear of Man

Lord, please teach me to fear You more than people.

Elijah had just witnessed God's astounding defeat of Baal's false prophets when he received Queen Jezebel's death threat. Scripture says he "was afraid and ran for his life." He isolated himself, traveled into the desert, slumped under a tree, and prayed to die (1 Kings 19:1-4).

"Fearing people is a dangerous trap, but trusting the LORD means safety," says Proverbs 29:25 (NLT). How true this is! Fearing people trapped Elijah in despair. It can do the same to us.

It can also trap us in disobedience. God gives us a specific task, but the fear of appearing inadequate to others hinders us from saying yes.

And then there's the trap of codependent behavior. The fear of triggering a negative response causes us to keep silent and let inappropriate behavior continue.

God has not given us a spirit of fear, so why are we afraid? He's bigger than any problem or person we'll ever face, and He's on our side. Therein lies courage.

Take Action: Read Psalm 27:1-3. Meditate on this truth: "The Lord is my light, my salvation, and my stronghold."

No Surprises

Lord, I rest in knowing You know all.

A diagnosis stuns us. An email leaves us speechless. A phone call flips our world upside down.

We make plans for our day, but within hours or even minutes, those plans are blown to smithereens and life takes a direction we hadn't anticipated. Sound familiar?

I suffered a severe foot injury while writing this book. A week later, the opposite knee developed issues that required surgery. With four book deadlines pressing, I could have panicked, but I felt only peace.

I found consolation in knowing my situation was no surprise to God. He knew about the deadlines, and He foresaw my physical challenges. He didn't wake up one morning and say, "Oh, goodness! What happened to Grace?"

"No human wisdom or understanding or plan can stand against the LORD," says Proverbs 21:30 (NLT). Our plans might change in a heartbeat, but rest assured that the sovereign God is not surprised.

We needn't panic or be afraid. God knows all about our situation, and He has everything under control.

Take Action: Pray aloud, "God, I believe nothing takes You by surprise. Help me trust Your sovereignty and rest in Your care."

Something Good About Suffering

Lord, thanks for lessons learned through suffering.

Everything seems to have an upside. Even suffering. The apostle Paul discovered this truth on his missionary travels. "We were crushed and overwhelmed... We expected to die. But as a result, we stopped relying on ourselves and learned to rely only on God, who raises the dead" (2 Corinthians 1:8-9 NLT).

Paul's situation looked hopeless, but there was an upside. By reaching the end of himself and his abilities, he learned to rely on God and His infinite resources. Then he experienced God's deliverance and, no doubt, inner rest by entrusting himself fully to the Father's care.

Perhaps you've experienced a family tragedy, a business setback, or a physical challenge. Maybe circumstances have stripped you of reliance on your own resources. It's looking bleak, but don't despair. Your situation has an upside—it's an opportunity to grow and to experience God in a new way.

What might that be?

Take Action: Describe a recent or current challenge in one sentence. Then fill in the blank: "But as a result, I learned _____."

Discipline

Lord, do what's necessary to make me holy.

The word "discipline" carries a negative connotation, but that's probably because it's often confused with punishment. Let's set the record straight.

Discipline is training that corrects, molds, or perfects the mental faculties or moral character. Punishment is a penalty or sanction given for a crime or offense. Proverbs 3:11-12 refers to the former—"My son, do not despise the LORD's discipline, and do not resent his rebuke, because the LORD disciplines those he loves, as a father the son he delights in."

Parents understand the importance of discipline. Without it, kids naturally display self-centered behavior, and trouble ensues. But when discipline is properly administered, they mature into responsible adults.

Sometimes we act like unruly kids, and our behavior warrants training that corrects. God, our heavenly Father, rightfully steps in to show us where we're wrong and teach us otherwise. We might feel He's unkind or unfair at times, but the opposite is true. He cares about our well-being because He delights in us. He desires our maturity and holiness.

Take Action: How do you respond when God disciplines you? Ask Him to give you His perspective.

His Purposes

Lord, I rest in Your sovereignty over my life.

Do you sometimes feel as if God needs your help to fulfill your life's purpose? Resist the urge, my friend.

Rushing to God's aid leads only to trouble, as we see in Sarah's life. She grew impatient as she waited for Him to deliver the son He promised, so she arranged for her husband to sleep with her servant Hagar. In their culture, children born from that union belonged to her.

Sure enough, Hagar conceived and delivered Ishmael, but the story unfolded like a soap opera. If only Sarah had trusted God to do what needed to be done (Genesis 16:1-6; 21:1-21).

We often stew when things don't go as we wish, but why? God's role is to coordinate details and divine appointments. Our role is to trust Him and joyfully submit to His way of doing things.

"I cry out to God Most High, to God who will fulfill his purpose for me," wrote the psalmist (Psalm 57:2 NLT). Let's recall these words when we feel anxious or impatient.

God will fulfill His purpose because He is who He is. Rest.

Take Action: Write "God will fulfill His purpose for me" on a recipe card. Post it on your fridge.

Give Glory

Lord, my heart's desire is to glorify You.

Listening to stories about God's activity in people's lives always brings spiritual encouragement. Some tell of deliverance from addictions. Others speak of broken marriages restored, adoptive adults being reunited with biological parents, miraculous healings, divine appointments, or last-minute financial provisions.

Details differ from one account to the next, but one thing remains constant—God receives glory when we recall and celebrate His goodness. This is especially true when our story shows His faithfulness in the midst of trials. "Call on me when you are in trouble, and I will rescue you, and you will give me glory," says Psalm 50:15 (NLT).

Sometimes we fail to give God glory because we are afraid of speaking publicly or we feel our story doesn't matter much. It's not as exciting as some, so who cares?

God does.

Stories about His involvement in our lives matter. Our experience might minister deeply to a particular individual. Perhaps it will renew hope and restore courage as she considers God's offer to help her too.

God deserves to receive honor. Let's be ready and willing to do our part.

Take Action: Ask God to glorify Himself through your story.

The Gift of Prayer

Lord, help me consistently give the gift of prayer.

Prayer is the best gift you can give a friend, especially when she's experiencing a change or a crisis. Your intercession will carry and support her when she doesn't have the strength to pray. And it will make a difference in the outcome of her situation.

The apostle Paul appreciated the prayers the Corinthian believers offered on his behalf. He wrote, "He will continue to rescue us. And you are helping us by praying for us. Then many people will give thanks because God has graciously answered so many prayers for our safety" (2 Corinthians 1:10-11 NLT).

Do you have a friend in need today? Ask her for specific requests. Don't just say you'll pray for her—do it with her when she expresses her concerns. Pray briefly over the phone for her, or email a prayer when the Holy Spirit brings her to mind. She can print it and reread it as often as she desires.

Give the gift that keeps on giving. Your friends will love you for it.

Take Action: Write a friend's name and needs on a recipe card. Carry it with you as a reminder to pray for her.

Overflowing Joy

Lord, thanks for showing me the secret to a joy-filled life.

Some people radiate joy. One gal I know suffers chronic back pain, but she always wears a smile. Another is greatly concerned for her son's safety in his new job as a police officer, but she encourages everyone she knows. One of my neighbors is losing her vision, but joy is her trademark.

What's their secret?

These women are doing what Jesus said. "When you obey my commandments, you remain in my love…I have told you these things so that you will be filled with my joy. Yes, your joy will overflow!" (John 15:10-11 NLT).

My friends experience joy because they're obeying God's commands. They trust Him at all times, they cast their burdens on Him, and they thank Him for the inner strength and peace He gives.

Joy doesn't come through rosy circumstances. It comes from obeying the One who knows how we best flourish. When our joy lacks, we'd do well to look at our spiritual self and ask, "Am I walking in obedience to Christ in all things?"

Take Action: Fill a glass of water to overflowing. Ask God for an obedient heart so that you might experience overflowing joy.

Faith

Lord, teach me to walk by faith.

Walking by faith creates white knuckles. Perhaps that's how Joshua felt when God commanded the Israelites to cross the Jordan River during flood season.

Ordering the priests to go and stand in the river may have seemed ludicrous to Joshua, but by faith, he relayed the command to them anyway, believing God would part the waters so they wouldn't drown. And He did—but not before they put their feet in the water (Joshua 3:8-16).

Faith is the anticipation of things unseen. Living with this attitude is a necessary part of the Christian life because "without faith it is impossible to please God" (Hebrews 11:6). God wants us to trust Him, and that trust is best demonstrated when we obey His marching orders implicitly.

Consider yourself blessed when God asks you to do something that requires faith. He's giving you an opportunity to grow spiritually and to see Him do amazing things on your behalf.

Sure, your knuckles may turn white in the process, but you'll honor and please God with your obedience.

Take Action: Memorize 2 Corinthians 5:7—"We live by faith, not by sight."

Accepted

Lord, thank You for satisfying my need to belong.

People have an innate yearning to be accepted or to belong. That desire can prompt us to buy the right car, wear the right clothes and accessories, and live in the right neighborhood even though these things surpass our budget. It can cause us to engage in inappropriate relationships or in behaviors opposed to God's standard of holiness. It can drive us to perfectionism.

Satan loves to capitalize on our yearnings by convincing us that we're not enough, we're unlovable, and we must somehow earn acceptance.

Truth is, we are accepted. Scripture tells us that God loves us and chooses us. "God decided in advance to adopt us into his own family by bringing us to himself through Jesus Christ. This is what he wanted to do, and it gave him great pleasure" (Ephesians 1:5 NLT).

Others may reject us, but God accepts us—and with great pleasure! We belong to Him. We're home.

Take Action: Memorize Ephesians 1:6 (NLT)—"We praise God for the glorious grace he has poured out on us who belong to his dear Son."

Truth or Trash

*Lord, please give me an insatiable appetite
for Your truth.*

A wise person is hungry for knowledge, while the fool feeds on trash," says Proverbs 15:14 (NLT).

Mankind is created with a hunger for spiritual reality. We choose whether to satisfy that appetite with godly truth or nibble on the trash our society serves up.

Society's buffet entices us with yummy-looking delectables. Follow your heart, the menu says. Stuff yourself with whatever tickles your emotional taste buds. The woman who partakes from that table eats trash that will make her spiritually sick. She's a fool, Scripture says.

But wise is she who recognizes its dangers and indulges in truth from God's word instead. This woman acknowledges Jesus Christ—the way, the truth, and the life—as Savior. She feasts regularly on those things that truly satisfy her spiritual needs and ensure her well-being—Christian fellowship, Bible study, worship music, service opportunities, and more.

What's in your spiritual diet? Are you feasting on the truth, or are you feeding on trash?

Take Action: Ask God to give you an insatiable desire for His word. He'll answer with a yes.

Anticipation

Lord, my mind cannot fathom the joys ahead.

Our family takes a vacation together for several days each summer. I always look forward to the fun we'll have and the memories we'll make. That anticipation gives me an inner boost when I'm feeling overworked and weary in the months prior. Knowing what's coming enables me to press on.

Imagine, then, the inner boost we can receive from knowing that heaven awaits. Imagine meeting Jesus face-to-face, looking into His eyes, and seeing His smile. Imagine entering the place He's prepared, where pain and death do not exist. Where sorrow, evil, and darkness are unknown. A place beyond human imagination, where God's glory dwells.

"So we don't look at the troubles we can see now; rather, we fix our gaze on things that cannot be seen. For the things we see now will soon be gone, but the things we cannot see will last forever," wrote the apostle Paul (2 Corinthians 4:18 NLT).

Days might be long and difficult sometimes, but heaven is coming. Joy lies ahead. Let that truth refresh you and give you strength to press on.

Take Action: Write "Heaven Is Coming" on a recipe card. Add a smiley face. Use it as a bookmark.

Relationship Clues

Lord, teach me to relate rightly to You and to people.

Our relationships with God and with man are directly linked. If we're experiencing problems with the latter, we should check for a problem with the former.

For instance, our desire to mask our weakness might indicate a fear that God will reject us if we don't measure up. But understanding His love for us frees us from the fear of man's rejection and enables us to be transparent.

Our need to control indicates an inability to trust God with the details of our lives. Understanding His sovereignty frees us from worry and enables us to let go.

Our inability to forgive reveals that we don't comprehend God's grace in our own lives. Understanding His forgiveness and His role as Judge enables us to extend grace to others.

"Everyone who loves the father loves his child as well. This is how we know that we love the children of God: by loving God and carrying out his commands," says 1 John 5:1-2. A healthy vertical relationship results in healthy horizontal relationships. If there's a problem, read the clues.

Take Action: Identify an interpersonal relationship struggle. What might be the root cause?

A Gift

Lord, I accept this gift You've offered me.

We give gifts for special occasions, such as birthdays, Christmas, and anniversaries. Sometimes we give gifts for no reason at all except that we want to show the recipient that we love him.

Jesus Christ has given us a gift because He loves us. When His life on earth was over and the time came for Him to return to heaven, He said, "I am leaving you with a gift—peace of mind and heart. And the peace I give is a gift the world cannot give. So don't be troubled or afraid" (John 14:27 NLT).

A gift is offered, and the recipient chooses whether to accept and open it. In the spiritual realm, Jesus—the Prince of Peace—offers the gift of peace to us, and we choose whether we will accept it.

When life's storm winds blow, remember this—peace is possible because Jesus has given it to us through relationship with Himself and through His promises. If we're not experiencing His peace, what might the reason be?

Take Action: Memorize John 14:27. Recall it when feeling anxious, and thank Jesus for the gift.

Cease Striving

Lord, thank You for taking responsibility for me.

A friend and her pastor husband sensed God changing their direction. They applied for a couple of ministry positions overseas, but nothing came of those. Finally he applied to take further studies at a seminary two provinces away.

Those doors flew open. Within six weeks, they visited the new city and found housing, sorted and packed their belongings, sold their house, bid family and friends goodbye, and transplanted their family of five.

Stories like this encourage our faith. They remind us that God is in control of everything concerning us and that we needn't worry or fear. He works on our behalf while we do our part, and He often exceeds our expectations.

A natural tendency is to stress over unknowns. This happens when we assume responsibility that ultimately rests with God. He offers this counsel to anxious hearts: "Be still, and know that I am God" (Psalm 46:10).

Beautiful.

Changes and challenges are parts of life. Let's remember that He is God in the midst of them, and we'll know peace.

Take Action: Breathe deep. Exhale and say, "I will be still and let You be God in my situation."

I Can Do Nothing

Lord, I need You desperately.

Having both legs incapacitated for three months made it impossible for me to do many activities I'd previously taken for granted, such as climb into bed or the shower, go outside, drive, and go grocery shopping. I depended on my husband's help for the simplest tasks. Jesus' words suddenly took on new meaning— "Apart from me you can do nothing" (John 15:5 NLT).

Christ's words say it all. We often go on our merry, self-sufficient way, forgetting that we are actually completely dependent on God for everything. Apart from His favor, each of us would be a sorry mess. Think about it—we can't even inhale our next breath without His nod.

An independent streak runs through us. It insists that we can do life on our own, thank you. But that mentality is contrary to God's word, and it lands us in trouble.

Let's agree with God that apart from Him we can do nothing. Doing so sets us free to discover the joy of experiencing His all-sufficient power. Why would we want anything less?

Take Action: Thank God that you can do all things through Him who strengthens you (Philippians 4:13).

Self-Control

Lord, thanks for the safety net of restraint.

Self-control entails discipline. It's one of the fruits of the Holy Spirit, and exercising it benefits us in numerous ways.

Practicing self-control prevents us from yelling at our kids when they've taxed our patience. It keeps us from criticizing our spouses and gossiping about the neighbors. It halts us from eating unhealthy foods and from eating and drinking more than our body needs.

Exercising self-control keeps our thought life and moral behavior pure. It enables us to say no to temptation so we can live without regrets. How many times have you lacked self-control and regretted the fallout later?

"The fruit of the Spirit is…self-control…Since we live by the Spirit, let us keep in step with the Spirit," says Galatians 5:22-25. When we allow the Spirit to fully control us, we gain the inner strength to say no to inappropriate human desires that tug our hearts. We are no longer enslaved to sinful or harmful desires.

We are free.

Take Action: In what part of your life do you need to exercise more self-control? Invite the Spirit to fully control you in that area.

Thank You

*Lord, grant me a thankful heart
for the kindness people have shown me.*

Friends have showered me with get-well gifts recently—cards, meals, potted plants, floral bouquets, and even a chocolate bar all the way from Germany.

I'm thankful for these displays of kindness, and I respond with a note of gratitude. These folks have made an effort to serve my family and me, and they deserve recognition for what they've done.

God's word tells us to honor those who deserve recognition. "Give everyone what you owe them...if revenue, then revenue; if respect, then respect; if honor, then honor" (Romans 13:7).

The list of people who have shown kindness to you and me could extend a long, long way. It would include pastors and their wives, youth sponsors, teachers, coaches, summer camp counselors, coworkers, neighbors, and even our hair stylists, to name a few. Imagine the encouragement these folks would feel if we took a moment to write a thank-you to express gratitude for their services.

Let's honor them. It's the right thing to do.

Take Action: Think of someone who has shown kindness to you and write a thank-you note. This can be someone from your past, such as a teacher who inspired you.

Worthless Worry

Lord, please forgive me for doubting Your character.

Some researchers say that only 8 percent of the things we worry about come to pass. That means we waste a ton of energy and time on the other 92 percent. And for what?

"Do not worry about your life," Scripture tells us. "Can any one of you by worrying add a single hour to your life?" (Matthew 6:25,27). Great advice! When we worry about things we can neither change nor control, we only shorten our lives and make ourselves miserable. So why do we do it?

I suspect we worry because we lack an understanding of God's character and promises. We do well to think about who He is and how this affects us. He is love; therefore we can trust Him. He is faithful; therefore we can trust Him. He is wise; therefore we can trust Him. He is ever-present; therefore we can trust Him. He is all-knowing; therefore we can trust Him. We doubt the character of a God so magnificent, and the result is worry.

God, grant us a greater understanding of who You are.

Take Action: What characteristic of God means the most to you today and why?

New Beginnings

Lord, I'm grateful for hope amid disappointment.

The disciples thought the end had come when Jesus' body was laid in the tomb. In reality, His death was only the beginning.

The end, as they supposed it to be, was painful but necessary. Christ's resurrection and His eternal victory over sin and death could not have happened without it.

Sometimes disappointments cause us to feel as though the end has come. A job layoff, a home foreclosure, a divorce, the death of a loved one, or the death of a dream—these things happen, and they leave us hanging. What now? What next?

Endings may feel final. When they come, turn your disappointment into anticipation by asking yourself, "What is God going to bring from this?" Surrender, pray, and wait to see what He'll do.

The Lord has a plan, and He unfolds it in His time and way. "The old order of things has passed away. He who was seated on the throne said, 'I am making everything new!'" (Revelation 21:4-5).

Watch. Be patient. Be amazed.

Take Action: Recall an ending you've experienced. What unforeseen beginning did it birth?

Fight the Good Fight

Lord, keep me faithful to You.

The apostle Paul endured shipwreck, snakebites, whippings, imprisonments, and more because of his faith in Christ. Lesser men might have turned their backs on God, but not Paul. His divine encounter turned him into an undeterred Jesus follower. Shortly before his death, he said, "I have fought the good fight, I have finished the race, I have kept the faith" (2 Timothy 4:7).

We can make the same claim someday too. Doing so is possible when we remember what Christ has done on our behalf. He sacrificed His life so we might live. Such fierce love deserves nothing less than undivided devotion.

Finishing well is also possible when we focus on God's purpose for our lives. Forget distractions and petty differences. Refuse to be sidetracked or bogged down in lesser things. Press on to win the prize for which God has called you (Philippians 3:12-14). Persevere, knowing His presence is with you. And push forward, anticipating His commendation—"Well done, good and faithful servant."

Take Action: Surrender anything—an inappropriate relationship, unforgiveness, fear—that might hinder your race. Ask God to give you the courage and strength to run well.

Notes

1. Michael Youssef, *Empowered by Praise* (Colorado Springs, CO: Waterbrook Press, 2002), p. 4.

2. Max Lucado, *Just Like Jesus: A Heart Like His* (Nashville, TN: Thomas Nelson, 2013), p. 125.

3. Max Lucado, *Everyday Blessings: 365 Days of Inspirational Thoughts* (Nashville, TN: Thomas Nelson, 2004), p. 366.

4. Catherine Marshall, *God's Promises Day by Day* (Nashville, TN: Thomas Nelson, 2003), p. 107.

5. Oswald Chambers, *My Utmost for His Highest* (Grand Rapids, MI: Discovery House, 1995), February 18 reading.

About the Author

Grace Fox is a speaker at
women's events internationally.
To book Grace for your next retreat or conference,
email her at
grace@gracefox.com

You can also follow Grace on Twitter at
@gracelfox or connect with her online at
www.gracefox.com
www.gracefox.com/blog
www.fb.com/gracefox.author

More Great Harvest House Books from Grace Fox

10-Minute Time Outs for You and Your Kids

Scriptures, Stories, and Prayers You Can Share Together

Grace provides engaging stories, activities, and prayers in a welcoming format to help you and your children share the riches of God's word together.

Moving from Fear to Freedom

A Woman's Guide to Peace in Every Situation

Grace demonstrates how you can face your fear and actually let it be a catalyst for change. She outlines "the upside of fear": When we stop hiding from God and instead cry out to Him for help, He answers, and we experience Him in new ways.

Peaceful Moments to Begin Your Day

Devotions for Busy Women

In this lovely padded hardcover, Grace invites you to delight in your faith by nurturing your relationship with God each day. In these encouraging devotions, you will encounter inspirational stories, Scripture-based prayers, and engaging meditations that lead you to the grace, comfort, and wisdom of God's presence.

To learn more about Harvest House books and
to read sample chapters, log on to our website:

www.harvesthousepublishers.com

HARVEST HOUSE PUBLISHERS
EUGENE, OREGON